Cover page

Splitting Pennies

Understanding Forex

Author:
Joseph James Gelet
Elite E Services, Inc.
www.startelite.com

Publishing information

Copyright © 2016 by Joseph James Gelet, Elite E Services, Inc.
Publisher: Elite E Services, Inc.
First Printing: March, 2016
Version: Original Master 13.2
Edition: US Trade – Createspace 6x9
ISBN: 153333109X
ISBN 13: 9781533331090
Produced in: Microsoft Word 2013
Number of Pages: 250
Date of Publishing: March 15th, 2016
Cover Artwork: Benjamin May
Website: www.splittingpennies.com
Email: info@fxrequest.com

Ordering Information:

Special discounts are available on quantity purchases by corporations, associations, educators, and others. For details, contact the Publisher Elite E Services at www.startelite.com or by email info@fxrequest.com

More information on ordering, quotation, references, or other SP related topics, visit www.splittingpennies.com

Table of Contents

Contents

Acknowledgements

This book is dedicated to my lovely wife Liudmila, my inspiration.   Without her this book would not be possible.

This book is the manifestation of 15 years hard work in Forex, recently manifested through a Forex case by Steinmeyer Law   www.steinmeyerlaw.com.   The support of my business partner and friend Randall Steinmeyer have been critical to this book, such as ideas and perspectives of how the financial system works from a legal perspective.

This book is possible because of my 15 years hard work in Forex. For the purpose of research and referencing, I've found many on related topics that I've decided to read which will take many years. But practically, if I had for example spent 15 years reading instead of working, the book would have a more referenced and intellectual character – but wouldn't have such unique experiences and perspectives as I've encountered in the business world. So I believe that although much evidence presented in anecdotal; it is even more valid, and valuable as such.   Because Forex is so new and unexplored.

This book is written with an American perspective by purpose.

Thanks to all writers of Forex books, articles, and other materials which have contributed to the knowledge presented here.

Read, read, read, read, read! No one ever does, of course. I have said it numerous times and it is ignored. It is a symptom of the following malaise:

Americanitis – a common mental deficiency in Americans, one that either prevents them from reading a legal contract, or causes them to believe only what they choose to about that contract, before it is signed.[i]

Thanks to Wikipedia, which has revolutionized how knowledge is created and distributed. Although I knew that by using Wikipedia as a reference it would undermine the credibility of the book; in the case of this topic which is so scarcely researched; Wikipedia is an excellent if not the best Forex reference – especially for rare economic theories, and political events not otherwise highlighted in the texts of history. A portion of the proceeds of this book will be donated to Wikipedia.

Finally, I would like to thank all readers of this book.

By reading this book – you'll know more than a Harvard MBA about Forex!

Preface

Forex is the largest business in the world dollar for dollar that no one understands. The supposition of this book is that Forex is the driver of the global economy, and we need to integrate it into our thinking, both for our own benefit and to protect ourselves from potential risks. When we think of 'offshoring' we think of shrewd corporations hiring non-American workers at pennies on the dollar. This is true – but what makes it possible, is Forex. The reason they do this, it's because of Forex, not because of US labor laws.

Another example, problems with debt, and US debt in particular. It's a concern for businesses, individuals, and politicians. But the US Dollar is a debt based currency, so by paying off all US debt it would obliterate the money supply. We've experienced massive progress, R&D, and innovation across most fields, but finance, and especially Forex; lag behind. We use financial regulations on a model that was built in 1915 and 1933. Imagine if we all drove cars from 1933 or used telephones from 1933.

This book is meant for both the unwashed and unenlightened, as well as financial professionals. The take away from this book should be a new part of the brain previously filled with knowledge about the current global financial system and how you can use this to grow your own portfolio.

The doctrine is that Forex per se is a complex system, and to understand this system we can only evaluate history through the perspective of monetary policy. The only source of any currency in this system is the central bank. What happens in between, is largely – irrelevant.

The writing style of this book is ad-hoc. Any acronym, is adjacent to explanation. Some hyperlinks left in the electronic document, but all significant references in the Appendices. Copied text from online sources is always referenced and *in italics*.

Bold letters and <u>underlines</u> are used to highlight key phrases that stand out from the rest of the text. To calculate the price of the book, we used an inflation calculator to determine the 2015 value of $1 in 1970. **It's $6.11** – or about 510.9% inflation – and that's according to the Fed!

THIS BOOK IS FOR UN-SOPHISTOCATED INVESTORS. BY READING THIS BOOK IN ITS ENTIRETY, YOU CAN CONSIDER YOURSELF A SOPHISTOCATED FOREX INVESTOR (SFI).

Good luck! May the pips be with you!

1: Forex in Perspective

The big question we must tackle first; **what is Forex?** We all have heard words like "Forex" and "FX Markets" and "Currencies" but often have misplaced associations. Now we'll rewire your brain a little by placing the axons to the correct synapses. ***Don't worry – it won't hurt!***

Forex fact: Every single person in the world is a Forex trader; if you have ever went to the grocery store and bought a loaf of bread and paid with currency (This would be known in Forex as the Bread/Dollar pair, or BRD/USD). If there is economic activity, Forex is involved. It is because Forex relates to the value of money itself. The Forex market determines also the value of products bought at the local shop, international trade balances, government debt, the value of a plethora of financial instruments, derivative markets, and literally – **every single financial transaction on the known planet Earth.**

Next time you hear "Forex" – don't think about abstract concepts or sinister bankers smoking cigars plotting how to rob clients; think about the change in your pocket. Think about how much it costs today to buy a pound of beef or a loaf of bread vs. 10 or 20 years ago. Think about all the foreign products you buy every day. With few exceptions (such as North Korea) every country in the world currently participates in the international trade system. It is even confusing to know what product is from what country. One of Ford motor company's most sophisticated factories is located in Brazil. Korean car manufacturers such as Hyundai and Kia manufacture cars in Alabama, USA.

Truly, the idea of the 'nation-state' is becoming more and more obsolete. But let's face it, it hasn't been reinvented for hundreds of years. What is a country at all, if not a currency? In the documents that create nations, their constitutions, always there is a 'right to create money' – but 28 countries in Europe chose to forgive this right, to participate in a larger economic super state, called "The European Union" which uses the "Euro" currency. A similar situation happened in "The United States" when the original 13 sovereign countries combined to create a super state that is the USA we know today.

When asking the question 'what is a currency' we should be asking in the reverse – what is a country? **A country is a currency.** What makes the United States a powerful country? The widespread global use of the US Dollar. When people trade countries it's called immigration. But the modern electronic internet based Forex system allows currencies to be exchanged in nanoseconds over and over again, even automatically, without any human intervention. What drives this system is largely an intelligence of itself; the Forex market has become the world's first quasi artificial intelligence.

A look at the markets: What is a market?

Let's understand what a market is. A market is a place where value is determined and trade commences. To keep things in common perspective let's use a green market that sells vegetables. There are 2 common roles; buyers and sellers. The sellers, or the merchants, pay a fee to the 'exchange' where the market is located in order to interact with buyers in the process of price discovery and finally sale. Sellers have a simple goal: sell their product for the highest possible price. Although we do not see this process in front of our eyes, it happens. Wal-Mart uses one of the world's fastest supercomputers to operate its business (Bianco, 2006) and most importantly for Forex, calculate its prices. Wal-Mart is one of the most visible Forex traders in the world; the majority of products sold by Wal-Mart are in the United States of America in US Dollars, and the majority of products manufactured and purchased by Wal-Mart are outside of the United States of America in a currency *other than* the US Dollar. Consumers who frequent Wal-Mart are largely unaware of this, but nonetheless, they are subject to price changes. The most significant element in the calculations of these price changes, are the Forex markets.

Using the green market analogy, understand that there are many types of markets, and markets are all inter-connected. Wal-Mart itself is a market – although the prices change very slowly. In fact, the word "Mart" defined means:

> 1. *Market; trading center; trade center.*
> 2. *Building, center, or exposition for the sale of goods by manufacturersand wholesalers to ret ail merchants.*
> 3. *Archaic. A fair.[ii]*

The Wal-Mart name is a combination of the surname "Walton" and "Mart" – or "Walton's Market." Buyers in

Wal-Mart or green markets only see the final price. But every purchase that is made – is a transaction in the Forex market.

In order to provide products to buyers in Wal-Mart, they must first either manufacture these products, or buy them in bulk; and then transport them to Wal-Mart supercenters. When they buy products, Wal-Mart often pays in foreign currency. This is a common situation sometimes referred to as 'offshoring' – a business has a mix of domestic and international elements, unknown to the consumer. They make it completely transparent, that consumers can buy as many products as they want, not knowing of the Forex components that allow Wal-Mart to offer such great prices. Let's put it this way – without Forex, Wal-Mart wouldn't exist. If Wal-Mart had to rely on 100% American US based factories, employees, logistics, and other business tools, it wouldn't be able to offer such competitive prices on such a wide variety of products.

From one perspective, Forex put Wal-Mart in business. Forex keeps Wal-Mart competitive. Wal-Mart is one of the largest employers in the world, and also one of the largest Forex traders, both in terms of size but also numbers. It's a great example but there are many examples.

Another great example of an American company driven by Forex is McDonald's (MCD). McDonald's was originally 100% American, but as the brand grew, they discovered they are actually more popular outside of the US than domestically. Currently more than 60% of McDonald's revenue comes from outside the United States. But McDonald's isn't utilizing this great opportunity for profit, and isn't even protecting itself from the risks.

1.1 Splitting Pennies – an investors' perspective

Over the years, Elite E Services experienced a wide range of responses in explaining our Forex business to investors. One of the most colorful examples of regurgitated explanations from an investor:

"I understand... You are splitting pennies,"... thereafter our nickname "The penny splitters."

This understanding, after our standard mathematical explanation of leverage, pips, and how it's possible to make money in Forex by extremely small price movements. Since inception, the Euro currency quoted as EUR/USD has moved in the range of about .90 to 1.60 (1 euro to X USD).

Metaphorically speaking, Forex traders split a penny a thousand ways, a million times in a minute.

With respect, "Splitting Pennies" underestimates the nobility and global significance of the Forex market; as if it is some 'trick' that some smart people have discovered to exploit the system (such as the rounding exploit software in the movie "Office Space" that collects all rounding errors into a separate account). A fair understanding mathematically, it fails to approach the real issue at the heart of Forex; the real time management of the global economic system as a whole.

But just to demonstrate the relative intelligence of this understanding "Splitting Pennies" – here are some humorous mischaracterizations of our Forex business:

- Our job is to travel in between countries with bags of cash and exchange them for foreign currency
- We operate a kiosk at the airport exchanging physical foreign currency
- We collect as an investment old coins and banknotes with the expectation their value will rise
- Somehow (not sure how this conclusion was reached) we are affiliated with government spy agencies, and Forex is a means to achieve our mission

In many ways, bankers are penny splitters, as Wall St. continually invents more ways to invest and trade, often with derivatives created artificially. Also correct with this characterization, is from the prism that the financial services industry as a whole, is completely artificial. Banks need the economy, the economy doesn't need banks.

In fact, banks have stifled economic growth substantially by creating financial crisis and sucking real economic value from the economy.

What is 'real' and what is 'virtual' – open your eyes! Cars are real, machines are real, buildings are real, and people are real. Money is an abstraction, a mathematical concept. Bankers who have 'sold' the masses the concept that 'money is real' do this by issuing symbol ridden paper with fancy stamps and markings that give the unwashed and unenlightened something to hold in the material world, as a sign that they exist. "This is MY MONEY!" Actually, its property of the Federal Reserve, but it's being held in your hands.

The basis for understanding Forex first requires a little un-learning. The first lesson:

MONEY DOESN'T EXIST

Money is a financial concept, an idea – based on mathematics. You cannot eat money, burn money, it has no properties in the physical world. It is simply an idea. There are thousands of historical examples of differing ideas about money, ranging from large stones carried by the Yap islanders to the modern Bitcoin. Money is more a philosophy, a way of life, than it is an object. Money is not an investment, and you cannot invest with money. The current "Money" system that the US uses (and also many countries) is called a FIAT system, or in other words, 'value by decree' – because we said so. So George Bush was right when he famously characterized his posse as the 'reality based community[iii]' – reality is what they say it is, not what is written in books or observed by scientists. At least that is how the global financial system works, which is defined by the world reserve currency, the US Dollar. The US Dollar is valuable because the Fed says it is, and people believe it.

Take this simple example. Imagine you write 100 on a piece of paper and try to use it in the store. They will look at you strange or maybe call Police. But if you present a crisp $100 Bill, printed by the US Mint for the Federal Reserve, they will gladly accept your payment and provide change. You can try this experiment yourself (kids, please ask your parents' permission).

(See image comparison – a US $5 Federal Reserve Note vs. an artist rendition $5 Elite E Services' Money)

So what is "Money" really? There are thousands of kinds of money, ranging from Gold to energy, it could be said that Oil is money. Without getting into the semantics of the English language, money is meant to be a medium of exchange, not a store of value. Currently, the world uses a Fiat Money system:[iv]

Fiat money *is a* <u>currency</u> *established as money by government regulation or law. The term derives from the* <u>Latin</u> <u>fiat</u> *("let it be done", "it shall be") used in the sense of an order or decree. It differs from* <u>commodity money</u> *and* <u>representative money</u>. *Commodity money is created from a good, often a* <u>precious metal</u> *such as* <u>gold</u> *or* <u>silver</u>, *which has uses other than as a* <u>medium of exchange</u> *(such a good is called a commodity), while representative money simply represents a claim on such a good.*

Or, in other words – the value of the US Dollar is determined by belief of the words of the Fed & financial officials inside the US Government. Because people believe the US Government is credible, and trustworthy, the US Dollar has value. By itself, it has no other value – no more than the paper it is printed on. It costs about 5.7 cents to print a US Dollar bill. So there you go – the real value of a US Dollar! And for some reasons (security holograms and so on) the $100 costs a whopping 14.3 cents[v]!

The Fiat system used by all major economies is much a game of 'hot potato' – it is known that the value of any single dollar of any fiat currency is constantly deteriorating, one must quickly exchange it for something valuable in the hope of preserving value and building wealth. This is exacerbated by Fed policy of near zero interest rates, market interventions, and QE programs.

When we see the stock market soaring to new weekly highs, doubling of real estate prices in some markets, and double digit increases in the price of meat and food staples – this is not inflation caused by traditional supply and demand – it is the effect of the Fiat money system, and an influx of massive amounts of new money into the money supply.

At the heart of this system is Forex. Because each Central Bank can only create as much of its own currency as it wants. Meaning, the Fed cannot print Euros and the ECB cannot print Yen. So take the example of the QE program by the Fed – a nearly unlimited supply of US Dollars is created (tens of trillions). That money circulates into the banking system and is used in various ways. But the most basic trade that banks can do with this new free money – is to quickly buy other money (such as Euros) which may deteriorate its value at a slightly slower rate.

What is strange about the current state of affairs, each Central Bank has a rational policy to destroy the value of their own currency in order to boost export markets (or in other words, the REAL economy). This is a rational policy, but the net global effect is that each major currency is in a desperate race to destroy its own value – called 'competitive devaluation.'

What supports the US Dollar (USD)

There is at the end of the day, only one thing that supports the US Dollar, or any FIAT currency: **BELIEF & TRUST.** The only real currency in the financial world is TRUST.

It is ironic that the USA is now the only country in the world with nearly no Forex knowledge, because the USA has the most interesting Forex history in the world. Before the US Dollar, there were thousands of currencies used in America. Banks issued their own currency. The civil war, largely thought to be about slavery, was really about establishing a banker dominated government whereby a central bank could be established such as they had done in England and many other European countries at the time.

"Let us control the money of a nation, and we care not who makes its laws" was said to be a "motto" of the House of Rothschild.

Being that TRUST is the only real currency, American officials know that this TRUST needs constant support! The world loves America, when it is popular to do so. By using the most sophisticated propaganda machine ever created, America regains this trust every day. Foreigners are brainwashed to believe without question that the US Dollar is trustworthy. Through social programming such as Hollywood movies, music with hidden messages, radio campaigns "Voice of America" there is no room for doubt left in the small brains of these unsuspecting commoners. It's also good for sales of Coca-Cola products & McDonalds' profits.

The backup plan, if this doesn't work, is the US Military. The policy is "Use US Dollars, or we will bomb you." All major US Military conflicts post WW2 (World War 2) can trace their roots explicitly to the supporting of the US Dollar, directly or indirectly. Because the general populace doesn't understand Forex, recent wars were blamed on "oil" – which is partially true. Yes, the US and allies wanted to seize control of Iraq's oil assets. But there isn't really that much oil in Iraq – especially when compared to neighbors. It's more significant to support the Petro-Dollar system, which oil is only sold in US Dollars. This process of US foreign policy is outlined in great detail by John Perkins in his book "Confessions of an Economic Hit Man" – a must read for any Forex trader. As described by Perkins, *"first they send in the banks (IMF/World Bank) with unreasonable loans, then if that fails they send in the "Jackals" (CIA/Paramilitary) and finally if that all fails, they send in the US Army."* (Perkins, 2004) What this means, under the guise of 'helping people,' an Elite group through the IMF &

World bank provide high interest loans to impoverished countries; usually ending up with critical infrastructure when they default. If the local leadership refuses the loans, they may attempt to instigate a revolution, coup, or assassination. If that fails, then full scale military options can be explored. The process is so subtle and filled with so many en-passant nuances that looking from the outside, it is hard to see what is really going on. In each case, whether looking at Chile, Indonesia, Kazakhstan, Mongolia, Ukraine, Iraq, Libya, or others – the cultural methods used are vastly different but the end result is the same; American or European bankers end up with the critical infrastructure prize of their choosing. It can be oil, water, rare earth minerals, or a business market.

The American Empire is actually a well refined, pseudo proxy for the greatest colonial power of all time, the British Empire. To some degree, the British Empire was a future manifestation of the remanence of the Roman Empire. It seems that these ruling empires, who ironically have similar cultures & religions, keep taking the same form under different circumstances, in different parts of the world, when it is in fashion. The interesting parallel layer in the shift of power from Europe to America – from "York" to "New York" York, interestingly, was a fortified city founded by the Romans, surrounded by a "Wall." [Figure 1 Photo of York, England]

But the American Empire's global spoils are gargantuan; the British and the Romans of their prime would be jealous. For example, the Bush family recently bought nearly 300,000 acres of land in Paraguay on top of the largest water aquifer in the world; the Guarani Aquifer[vi]. This property alone could supply the entire world with water for 200 years. Carpetbaggers, or smart business? It's a logical investment, considering the rising cost of water, and the growing population, and how important it is for life on planet Earth. But the parallel here is that it resides not in Texas, a regulated land of high taxes and stiff politics; but in Paraguay, a land of foreign influence by the Americans, and specifically, the CIA[vii]:

The recent "institutional coup" against President Fernando Lugo of Paraguay reflects a long-standing desire by the U.S. Central Intelligence Agency (CIA) to prevent any candidate not reflecting the policies of Paraguay's entrenched oligarchy from ever attaining the presidency of that nation. According to a formerly SECRET CIA Directorate of Intelligence's Office of African and Latin American Analysis research paper, uncovered from the U.S. National Archives and dated August 1985, the CIA never planned for a non-member of the conservative Colorado Party from ever succeeding long-time Paraguayan dictator General

Alfredo Stroessner. The Paraguayan dictator, who ruled Paraguay from 1954 to 1989 with the backing of the CIA and the Pentagon, was one of America's staunchest Latin American allies. **Stroessner, a Colorado Party stalwart, supported the U.S. invasion of the Dominican Republic in 1965 and sent Paraguayan military officer to the infamous School of the Americas in Fort Benning, Georgia for training.** [viii]

Money doesn't exist, and money is worthless. But it can buy you a paramilitary operation, a nice little dictatorship in South America, and eventually the spoils of war: The Guarani Aquifer. The belief and trust in the US Dollar supports the American Empire, including all of its annexations; both official and private. And just to keep things in perspective, let's thank such entrepreneurs for doing so – because at the rate California is losing water, we'll soon need these resources back home! These guys are penny splitters too – they just use very big pennies!

Months before the actual invasion of Iraq, Saddam Hussein officially announced that oil would be priced in Euros[ix]. Of course, this single announcement alone was not the reason for Military deployment, it is simply an example of the trend in that time. It seems that such events and plans are often near, usually preceding, a major US invasion, presidential assassination, or other major game changing event. The Iraqi government was experimenting with ways to work outside of the US Dollar denominated system. Had the experiment had the opportunity to work, it could have spread to other nations that really do have huge oil reserves, and possibly ended the Petro-Dollar system. They had even considered using a regional currency backed by gold, the Arabic Dinar.

So like many mischaracterizations, it is only partially true that the Iraq war was about oil. It's partially true that the US Military is protecting 'freedoms' – the fact is the most powerful freedom the USA enjoys is the freedom to bomb other countries with virtually no retribution. This is the elephant in the room at the negotiating table. How is this connected to Forex? Because the US Dollar is the world reserve currency. All other currencies are backed by the US Dollar. And the US Dollar is backed only by belief & trust! (And the subtle threat that by not using US Dollars you might get bombed). These statements do not place judgement; simply explain the financial system that we currently choose to use on this small planet Earth. They say that the population deserves its rulers – this can never be more true than today. If you look at US foreign policy, the more cozy the US ally, the bigger user of US Dollars and US products.

The modern Forex system has become a tool for the enslavement of the population (That means – the enslavement of *the worker*). **Every day, you work for less and less wages.** There are no laws protecting consumers from this – because lawmakers mostly do not understand it. The hidden tax – inflation! It's a cozy relationship between Washington & Wall St., managed by the Federal Reserve Bank – a private institution. But this enslavement is not physical, it is virtual, and it is optional. It is allowed for anyone to open a Forex account and trade Forex. It's possible to utilize various Forex related tax advantages to increase your wealth. It's possible for anyone to hedge the declining US

Dollar – and the gallon of milk will cost in real terms adjusted for inflation the exact same amount today as in 10 years from now.

But, if you are a billionaire, institution, or have substantial financial assets, you are greatly benefiting from this system, as in recent years you've probably seen your portfolio balloon. So because the owners of society have benefited so greatly from this Forex system, there is no perceived need to do anything about it. In fact, it only solidifies the collective interest to keep the status quo as it is, and to keep the Forex system behaving as it is.

1.2 Practical Forex Trading examples

These examples have been practiced by Forex professionals & common people alike, for a number of reasons. They are not trade recommendations and these examples are not very useful today. But they serve as good examples of how anyone can profit from Forex even accidentally.

In the context of Forex understanding – **if you aren't gaining in Forex – you are certainly losing!**

The Tourist Trade – Seasonal FX patterns

Seasonal European tourism has always had an impact on regional currencies. Northern Europeans save their cash during the year and decide to migrate south during the winter for vacation. The North typically had more complex economies while the South developed less and still relied on tourism to supplement their income from farming and other subsistence businesses. We'll use the traditional example of German tourists visiting Greece. Because of the large amount of tourists exchanging currencies from Deutche Mark to Drachma, it would increase the price of Drachma. It would cost more and more DM to buy Drachma as the season went on. All season Harry Hotelogolopogous would collect these more valuable Drachmas but as the season passed, realizes that he needs new kitchen equipment for the café, which is only produced in Germany. Thus, Harry must spend some of his newly received Drachmas in Germany, and needs Deutche Marks. This drives the price of DM back up to where it was before the season. While these seasonal changes did not dictate the value of the currencies completely, there were noticeable patterns based on this simple economic activity, especially during the 70's, 80's, and 90's – before the widespread use of electronic trading, derivatives, and the Euro currency. Speculators could literally simply acquire the southern currency before the season, hold it, and sell it after. Southern Currencies in this trade included Italian Lira, Maltese Lira, Greek Drachma, and Spanish Peseta.

Islama-arb

This strategy was popular in the mid-2000 era when interest rates were still single digits in most countries. First, a little background on Islam and Sharia law[x]. The Islamic community uses Sharia Law, their code of principles and ethics which guide their lives. They follow this law by their own choice; it is not mandated by any state. However, many Islamic countries have passed legislation based on Sharia principles. It varies from country to country and is highly contested. For Forex the most interesting component is the prohibition of Riba[xi], or interest.

Riba is also applied to a variety of commercial transactions. Most Islamic jurists describe two kinds of Riba:

- *Riba an-nasiya: an excess (riba) charged for a loan in cash or kind.*

- *Riba al-Fadl: the simultaneous exchange of unequal quantities or qualities of a given commodity.*

Because of this, traditional Western investment is banned. Those who follow Sharia Law strictly, cannot invest in stock markets because listed companies use interest in their business. In the western world, nearly all investments are tied to interest. So for strict Muslims who follow Sharia Law, compliant investments are few.

Forex, as is commonly traded by the majority of banks in the world, uses the daily interest component called Rollover. Calculated annually and charged daily, it is paid or charged to your Forex account based on the swap rate of your existing position. The swap rates are provided to the clients per pair by the bank/broker where your account is. They are positive or negative depending on your position (long or short) and if the swap rate for that pair is positive or negative. For example if the prevailing interest rate per annum of the Euro is 2%, and the US Dollar 1%, and you are long EUR/USD (which means you are short the US Dollar), you would be net positive swap 1% (minus the small swap spread). This is divided by the number of days in the year and paid to your account, usually daily at 5pm Eastern Standard Time (EST). Because this rate is so small, Forex traders usually disregard this as it is irrelevant to the amount of money that can be made or lost on a Forex position. Although, there are some traders who even utilize the 5pm time to capture the swap payment.   Due to the strange rules of banks/brokers, most will calculate and pay this swap exactly at 5pm, such that if you buy 100,000 EUR/USD at 4:59pm EST and sell 1 minute later at exactly 5:00pm EST you would receive the swap payment.   Other brokers will have you wait another agonizing minute – until 5:01pm EST.   Then there are those rare old-school institutions that will actually close trading for 15 minutes, from 5pm – 5:15pm, to calculate their daily trading activities and prevent such opportunities. The rules at each institution are different.

Because of this rollover component, traditional Forex trading is also banned according to Islamic Law. But just as the great Mohammad has taken, he has also given – an opportunity for Sharia Banking! So to allow Muslims to trade Forex in compliance with Sharia Law, Sharia banks offer "Sharia Forex" which means there is NO ROLLOVER!

Immediately, many westerners opened accounts with these Sharia brokers. The strategy was simple. Go long GBP/JPY in your western account, short GBP/JPY in the sharia account, pocket the risk free difference. During the time, about 7%-8% per year return, guaranteed! Multiplied by leverage reasonably, about 100% per year, guaranteed! [Figure 2 Central Bank interest rates as of February 2016]

🏛 Central Bank Interest Rates (select bank from list)

Country	Rate	Country	Rate	Country	Rate
Australia	2.00% AUD	UK	0.50% GBP	Poland	1.50% PLN
Bulgaria	0.01% BGN	Hong Kong	0.75% HKD	Romania	1.75% RON
Canada	0.50% CAD	Hungary	1.35% HUF	Russia	11.00% RUB
Switzerland	-0.75% CHF	Israel	0.10% ILS	Sweden	-0.50% SEK
China	4.35% CNY	Japan	-0.10% JPY	Singapore	0.19% SGD
Czech Republic	0.05% CZK	Mexico	3.75% MXN	Turkey	7.50% TRY
Denmark	0.05% DKK	Norway	0.75% NOK	USA	0.50% USD
Eurozone	0.05% EUR	New Zealand	2.50% NZD	South Africa	6.75% ZAR

So what stopped this strategy from working? A number of things, most importantly that interest rates have fallen to near zero, and with high spreads and various transaction fees, it makes the strategy barely profitable. Exotics such as the Russian Ruble that pay 11% may not be offered by the Sharia broker. Currencies that pay .5% or even 2% would not make the strategy very profitable. Also, the Sharia brokers created new rules that these accounts should be only for proven Muslims. Some clients went through the trouble to convert to Islam, or find an Imam friend to open the account, but this is burdensome for the average Forex trader. To make this trade really complicated, some Sharia brokers now will charge a commission per trade, usually similar to the swap, thus making the trade break even or barely profitable. One FX hedge fund made an unknown amount of millions running only this strategy. Now, it would take a Forex bank to be able to execute this strategy. But if one is willing to go through all the red tape – it does represent risk free profit, as much as 100% per year.

While this strategy made a lot of money for a select few Forex traders for about 5 – 7 years, it is no longer valid for the average investor. However, it serves as a great example of unique opportunities that arise in

Forex that simply would not be possible in other markets.

Contrary to popular thinking on Wall St. there is a free lunch in Forex. The reason is that Forex is NOT a zero sum game. The supply of each currency, referred to as the money supply, is continually expanding. That means there is an ever increasing amount of money to be captured.

Deflated property in niche emerging markets

In the year 2000 the New Zealand Dollar was below .40 against the US Dollar (NZD/USD). During this time, the property market in New Zealand was severely depressed. During the 90's, New Zealand experienced a 'brain drain' of its best and brightest who suffered from 'island fever' and went to Europe, America, and Asia. It was possible to buy properties significantly below fair market value. From the perspective of the US Dollar which was strong, there was an additional 50% discount. Locally, *in New Zealand*, a NZD was the equivalent of $1 US Dollar. But the exchange rate was more than 2 to 1, giving American investors a huge advantage. To make things even better, New Zealand banks were paying up to 8% interest on basic savings accounts! And because of Forex tax rules, much of this profit was tax free! Also during this period (2000 – 2005) there was a real estate boom, and over a period of about 5 years, property prices nearly doubled. This, combined with the Forex component whereby the NZD/USD exchange rate went from .40 to over .80, provided a less than 5 year 400% return on their investment, nearly tax free. Forex tax rules are extremely complex and a topic for an entire chapter. Suffice to say that there are many tax benefits to Forex investing which do not exist in the accounting of one single functional currency. These rules are known by many Fortune 500 companies and utilized by companies such as Wal-Mart, making their effective tax rate much less. In fact, the use of offshore corporations in Bahamas, Caymans, and other jurisdictions, provides many Forex tax breaks, more than the jurisdiction does by itself.

Military Payment Certificates

A long forgotten instrument used during times of war, the MPC provided a way for the US Military to control their influence on the local economy (which was often significant). From Wikipedia:

Military payment certificates[xii], or MPC, was a form of currency used to pay U.S. military personnel in certain foreign countries. It was used in one area or another from a few months after the end of <u>World War II</u> *until a few months after the end of U.S. participation in the* <u>Vietnam War</u> *– from 1946 until 1973. MPC utilized layers of line* <u>lithography</u> *to create colorful* <u>banknotes</u> *that could be produced cheaply. Fifteen series of MPCs were created. However, only 13 series were issued. The remaining two were largely destroyed, although some examples remain.[1] Among the 13 released series a total of 94 notes are recognized.*

MPCs evolved from <u>Allied Military Currency</u> *as a response to the large amounts of* <u>US Dollars</u> *circulated by American servicemen in post-*<u>World War II</u> <u>Europe</u>. *The local citizens might not trust local currencies, as the future of their governments was unclear. Preferring* a stable currency like U.S. dollars, local civilians often accepted payment in dollars for less than the accepted conversion rates. Dollars became more favorable to hold, inflating the local currencies and thwarting plans to stabilize local economies. Contributing to this problem was the fact that troops were being paid in dollars, which they could convert in unlimited amounts to the local currency with merchants at the floating (black market) conversion rate, which was much more favorable to the GIs than the government fixed conversion rate. From this conversion rate imbalance, a black market developed where the servicemen could profit from the more favorable exchange rate.

To reduce profiteering from currency arbitrage, the U.S. military devised the MPC program. MPCs were paper money denominated in amounts of 5 cents, 10 cents, 25 cents, 50 cents, 1 dollar, 5 dollars, 10 dollars, and starting in 1968 20 dollars. MPCs were fully convertible to U.S. dollars upon leaving a designated MPC zone, and convertible to local currencies when going on leave (but not vice versa). It was illegal for unauthorized personnel to possess MPC, and that policy, in theory, eliminated U.S. dollars from local economies. Although actual greenbacks were not circulating, many local merchants accepted MPC on par with US dollars, since they could use them on the black market. This was especially evident during the Vietnam War when the MPC program was at its zenith. To prevent MPC from being used as a primary currency in the host country and destroying the local currency value and economy, MPC banknote styles were frequently changed to deter black marketers and reduce hoarding, as the old style would become worthless. Many veterans can recount a conversion day or C-Day.

C-days in Vietnam were always classified, never pre-announced. On C-day, soldiers would be restricted to base, preventing GIs from helping Vietnamese civilians—especially local bars, and other black market people—from converting old MPC to the newer version. Since Vietnamese were not allowed to convert the currency, they frequently lost savings by holding old, worthless MPC. People angry over their MPC loss would sometimes attack the nearest U.S. base the next night in retaliation. To illustrate the Vietnam War MPC cycle, in mid-1970, a GI could have a friend in the United States mail a $100 bill in standard U.S. currency, take it "downtown" and convert it to $180 MPC, then change the MPC to South Vietnamese piasters at double the legal rate. The soldier could then have a day shopping, bar hopping, or otherwise spending freely, paying in low-cost local currency, and finishing the day with a hefty profit. To continue the black market cycle, that $100 greenback would find its way to high-level Vietnamese government officials, especially the corrupt ones, who could travel out of country, where the U.S. currency could be deposited safely (Bangkok, Taipei, or Hong Kong). Rumors also suggested that this hard currency (US dollars), would find its way to North Vietnamese European exchange accounts. Thirteen series of MPC were issued between 1946 and 1973, with varied designs often compared to Monopoly money due to their colors. After the official end of U.S. participation in the Vietnam War in early 1973, the only place where MPC remained in use *was South Korea. In autumn of 1973, a surprise conversion day was held there, retiring MPC and substituting greenbacks. MPC was never again issued, and the concept lay dormant until the late 1990s, when it was revived somewhat in the form of the Eagle Cash stored value card system, used by U.S. armed forces in Iraq.*

"The cause of living in the past is dying right in front of us." – Gone with the Wind (Fleming, 1939)

1.3 Forex history lesson 1: pre-USD global politics

History is not only a great teacher, if we look at certain events through a set of Forex glasses, we can see a broader, clearer and simpler picture of Forex painted. To really understand Forex, we have to understand how we got to the current USD backed system of electronic trading we have today, and will likely have for the foreseeable decades to come.

We must understand pre-World War 1 global politics a little. This was a time of great change in the world. The industrial revolution fueled growth of industrial economies, led by Britain and the United States. Electricity, the automobile, the manufacturing process, innovations in medicine, communications, and countless other paradigm shift technologies changed every aspect of life in the western world. A new business climate needed financial markets to support them – most importantly the money market. With the advent of the telegraph, a 'wire payment' was possible. The Great British Pound Sterling is called 'cable' because of the undersea Atlantic cable laid between London and New York in 1866[xiii].

The Bank of England was established in 1694. The Federal Reserve in the United States was not established until 1913. Colloquially speaking, European bankers were more established, more organized, and more ahead of the game than the Americans. The American Civil War was a fight about Forex – not slaves. Slavery was a trade issue, and global trade was at stake. Contrary to popular belief, the Civil War had much international influence. Countries supported both sides for various reasons. At one point, the South produced 75% of the world's cotton[xiv]. Expanding colonial powers needed quality, cheap cotton (among other products) provided by the south. This was only possible with this deplorable practice; slavery. For this purpose, global economic powers supported both sides for various reasons. More importantly, European bankers wanted control of the financial system. America was a new market to exploit – with little financial training (as the Europeans had over a period of hundreds of years). The banking elite of Europe of that time really looked at America as a bunch of ruffians. But nonetheless, it was an emerging market! It was even rumored that JP Morgan was a front for Rothschild interests in America.

Control of the money supply is control of the economy. This is important because it distinguishes the issue of control vs. ownership. Much of the 'end the Fed' debate is over ownership. Who owns a central bank is irrelevant because – what will you do with it? Print money of course. Control of a central bank – i.e. choosing who gets the printed money, this is what the bankers fight for. We still do not know where the Fed sent Trillions of USD 'currency swaps' during the financial crisis of 2008. This too – is irrelevant. Because it is fully legal – this is the system that we use today in the world. It's important to understand that it is not a crime for the Federal Reserve to give money to its member banks – that is its job!

European bankers had a huge influence in establishing the Federal Reserve Bank. Fast forward to 2010, and the Fed's 'quantitative easing' program, sent Trillions of US Dollars to unknown European banks. During the Gilded age, robber barons and tycoons were making a fortune in industry, without a real solid banking system to support it. As this European influence reached America – they had a template. Actually they had many templates:

- Bank of Amsterdam, 1609
- Riksbank (Sweden) 1664
- Bank of England 1694

We can only surmise what was in the minds of European bankers at this time, but their agenda was clear. By establishing a single currency in America, they could not only control the US economy, but finance their operations in Europe. In this context, it is not ironic or surprising that the United States spent the next 100 years sending US Dollars to Europe in various ways and manners (i.e. the Marshall Plan, foreign aid, etc.). The best perspective for the understanding of Forex is to analyze the flow of money around the world. The central bank is the only primary emission of currency. New currencies such as Bitcoin are challenging that model. But currently, we are using a system created more than 400 years ago.

If you think this history is not important for your understanding of Forex – bear in mind that the dollar that underpins the modern Forex system – was created in 1913! Just imagine for a moment what life was like on planet Earth, in 1913.

1.4 The American Forex System

Richard Nixon effectively created the current, modern American Forex system by abandoning the Bretton Woods agreement and floating the US Dollar against other foreign currencies. This action was so unexpected, it was referred to as the Nixon Shock[xv]:

The Nixon Shock was a series of economic measures undertaken by United States President Richard Nixon in 1971, the most significant of which was the unilateral cancellation of the direct convertibility of the United States dollar to gold.

While Nixon's actions did not formally abolish the existing Bretton Woods system of international financial exchange, the suspension of one of its key components effectively rendered the Bretton Woods system inoperative. While Nixon publicly stated his intention to resume direct convertibility of the dollar after reforms to the Bretton Woods system had been implemented, all attempts at reform proved unsuccessful. By 1973, the Bretton Woods system was replaced de facto by a regime based on freely floating fiat currencies that remains in place to the present day.

Also importantly, Nixon froze prices and established an import duty on foreign items, to support the US economy. While Wall St. initially applauded Nixon's bold move, and the Dow rose 33 points on the news (at the time the biggest daily gain ever) – Nixon's profound economic effects would not be seen for another 30 years. But most importantly, and seemingly without the approval of the global ruling Elite – Nixon's move showed that an American President could unilaterally create a financial system by use of executive power. Of course, no one will ever know who Nixon met with at Camp David the weekend prior to the Nixon Shock. Nixon later admitted to rely heavily on the council of John Connally, former Texas Governor and who was wounded during the JFK assassination. Also ironically, just before JFK was assassinated he signed executive order 11,110 authorizing the US Treasury, not the private Federal Reserve Bank, to issue US government notes backed by silver[xvi]. Whoever or whatever forces were behind this significant financial event; Nixon took credit for it, Nixon enforced it, and it created the American Forex System.

For all practical purposes the world uses an American Forex System. This is because the US Dollar is the world reserve currency. Secondly but also important, the US is the global dominant military power. Third but very important, much of the world loves America and wants to do business with America, even if that means simply using US Dollars in their village. Most importantly however, the world trusts America (at least the allies do). For the time being though, this power is simply because there is no practical alternative. Europe now has a super currency but brought with it social unrest, hyper inflated debt and a myriad of economic problems. Asia is in complete disarray and certainly in no position to compete. That leaves only a young Russia to replace America as the global banking leader, but Russia is probably generations away from having a robust financial services system capable of playing such a global role (but in time – they will!).

In fact, of all the possible new potential players as a World Reserve backer, Russia is the long term front runner. A historically young civilization (little is known pre-8th Century AD[xvii]), Russia is now lean and mean and soon will have its chance to shine as economic and financial superpower. With the expansive growth of India, China, Brazil, and other EM (Emerging Markets) which are clearly beyond America's ability to manage, new management will naturally emerge which is culturally and logistically capable of handling this new generation that simply didn't exist before. China does not seem to be a serious candidate for this role, considering it cannot even manage itself. Other potential would-be players are bogged down in their own domestic issues.

Anyway, by the time the US Dollar is really dethroned from its reserve status, it will likely not be replaced by another country's currency, but rather, a new type of reserve system, such as a world currency or something with Block chain.

For the time being, the American Forex system serves its purpose, and will do so for far future. Because this system has created so much wealth for so many, there is a vested interest for them to keep it going as long as possible. And although there is still much talk about alternatives, it's just talk. There isn't any real competition to the US Dollar or even a hint that there will be in the future. Of course, anything can happen; the fall of the Roman Empire coincided with a debasement in their currency[xviii].

Nihil tam munitum quod non expugnari pecunia possit - No fort is so strong that it cannot be taken with money. (Cicero)

The current American Forex system has been in place for about 100 years, plus or minus, depending on how you calculate when it 'started.' This chart seen below is widely circulated by Dollar Bears, reminding us that life is short, even for a super power.

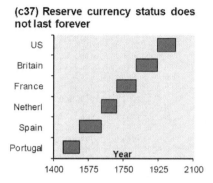

(c37) Reserve currency status does not last forever

While being the dominating global power that goes hand in hand with a global reserve currency has been in the hands of the major colonial powers France, Spain, Portugal, and the Netherlands; it was the British who stand out as the major global innovator and leader. The British have been at the cutting edge of global business and trade since their rise to power. They refined systems and trade routes, ways of doing business, and ways to manage a global empire. What the British did in India is particularly interesting, because some would argue that although the British 'occupied' India; they left India with more than when they came. Something such as the British Raj just wouldn't be possible in today's day and age. The British left their mark on global finance and even today, as the world uses the American Forex system, the capital of Forex is London, not New York.

London was perhaps always the center of modern Forex. In fact even in the hidden roots of American "capitalism," some argue, is that it was really British mercantilism in disguise (in other words, better marketing). The British were clever enough to use proxies such as The United States to do their own bidding, and this is especially important with Forex.

America is sort of a massive 'white label' for British interests. While on the surface, even during the Iraq war, it was joked that the reverse was true. Tony Blair was depicted as a 'tag along' doing whatever George Bush said. Well, as far as Forex goes – it's the London banks that call the shots. Some of the most significant Forex companies in the world are based in London, not New York. No one can argue against the global power of Wall St. – but in this majestic awe that we gaze before, we do not see the Forex reality, that a small handful of foreign banks control the Forex market though their London operations. Although we use an American Forex System, London still maintains the rank as #1 Forex hub in terms of total volume traded.

The American Forex system is a global financial Monopoly. The best example is the "Petro Dollar" trade. By pricing and selling crude oil in US Dollars, it guarantees a constant supply of buy orders for USD. This is a triple slam dunk for the global USD financial Monopoly:

1) Oil producing nations who want to participate in the Petro Dollar system buy USD naturally and invest much of those USD in US markets, US Treasuries, and other US denominated instruments. There could be no greater mechanism to support a currency, if one was to be constructed. Thanks Nixon!

2) By use of the USD, it virtually eliminates any competition (such as a Euro based or Ruble based system), thus ensuring more and more a USD dominant system. It also eliminates any 'would be' alternatives such as an Arabic Dinar

backed by gold, or other currencies that might be used by such economies.

3) Because other currencies are backed by the US Dollar, any financial attack on the US Dollar would also sink other currencies. While the Petro Dollar system isn't a currency, it means that Oil is effectively backed by dollars. Richard Nixon securitized a commodity that OPEC (Organization of the Petroleum Exporting Countries) has naturally at no cost to them. But this is ingenious, because although both USD and Oil is free to both countries; Oil needs to be extracted from the ground at a cost, and has limited supply. USD on the other hand, has no limit, costs nothing to manufacture electronically, and can be transported around the world instantly without cost of transport.

US Investors should thank Richard Nixon for creating this global economic Monopoly. What made the US economy strong for the past 40 years, more than any other factor, was the strength of the US Dollar. Although the US Dollar sank immediately after the Nixon shock and for subsequent years, it was followed by the 80's and 90's, considered by the majority of economists to be historically great economic periods. Fed policy as a driver of economic growth, would not have been so flexible and positive in later years (such as the Volcker period) if a fixed Bretton Woods exchange system was being used.

This can be reason number 29 why there is an anti-Forex policy, hidden and public, known and unknown, conscious and subconscious; in the USA. Because why should we encourage Forex trading, when we buy everything in US Dollars? In fact, why doesn't the whole world use US Dollars? Forex must be for countries with weak currencies, or cheese eating surrender monkeys. (Note the sarcasm)

In fact, the American Forex system is anti-competitive. It stifles any potential competition, and solidifies the USA's **Monopoly on money**. US Dollars (USD) really are 'Monopoly Money.'

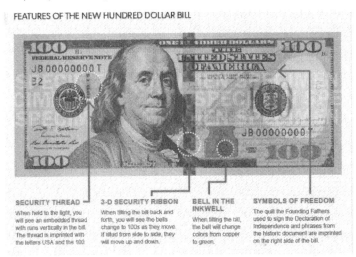

FEATURES OF THE NEW HUNDRED DOLLAR BILL

SECURITY THREAD
When held to the light, you will see an embedded thread with runs vertically in the bill. The thread is imprinted with the letters USA and the 100.

3-D SECURITY RIBBON
When tilting the bill back and forth, you will see the bells change to 100s as they move. If tilted from side to side, they will move up and down.

BELL IN THE INKWELL
When tilting the bill, the bell will change colors from copper to green.

SYMBOLS OF FREEDOM
The quill the Founding Fathers used to sign the Declaration of Independence and phrases from the historic document are imprinted on the right side of the bill.

2: The American Forex Delusion

Forex is all about paradox. In the Forex market for example, countries actually WANT their currency to go down, in order to boost their export markets. Imagine a stock issuer that was trying to invent ways for its stock price to collapse! It's very counterintuitive – but in Forex – this is common.

So now we will explore the irony, that in the largest economic power in the world, the United States, the global leader in financial innovation, Forex is the least utilized, and the least understood.

The American Forex Delusion – Article originally published on Zero Hedge by Global Intel Hub on 12/08/2015[xix].

Hitler said often that the bigger the lie, the easier it would be [for the masses] to believe. This is nowhere more significant than in Forex. Russia and America have similar demographics of people involved in Forex markets; both have extremely uneducated populations (even 'financial professionals' often have no clue about the ramifications of Forex), both have extremely polarized "Elite" (the bankers who run Forex) and the 'rest' who are left to have their savings eaten away by inflation. In fact, central banks have mandated the investing population - it's necessary to achieve above average returns just to break even.

We'll use Russia here as an example to contrast the US Forex market because they earned it - our new allies in the Middle East. This is Russia's first role as world policeman in Syria (as the "New Russia") and anytime a superpower such as Russia or America invades and bombs another country, there will be angry people (i.e. blowback). But, such situations often bring together unusual allies; the circumstances create allies (in this case, a common enemy Muslims/Islamic state) as did World War 2 and many other similar situations.

Let's quickly look at some of the biggest lies promulgated by the Elite. Who are "They"? Well, you can read about "them" here, here, and here. Why they do it, should be no question. It has allowed them to develop a global tech economy nearly for free (on the backs of the worker), and at the same time amass a fortune never before seen in known modern human history. All of this is possible due to lack of knowledge and education, or in other words, their ability to sell these lies to the population (by the way, Propaganda was invented by an American Edward Bernays; many of the methods used by Hitler, Stalin, and others are now being used by corporate America).

Over a period of more than 75 years, the Elite have invested billions of dollars and have a proven track record for brainwashing the population, in all countries, but most notably in America and in Russia (although with different cultural motives).

Lie #1: Inflation is caused by supply and demand, and other natural economic forces

This is the biggest lie that allows the real owners of the global financial system to fleece the population of their assets. Slavery is illegal, but working 80 hours a week for just enough money to pay for your housing, food, and health for your family, is not existence. It's the new slavery. You see, during the industrial revolution the Elite learned that physical chains were no longer necessary. By promoting such anti-values as gluttony, ignorance, apathy, and by promoting the Ego (i.e. Facebook "Look at me!) - It would allow the Elite to easily convince workers to run on the mill like lab rats for almost no pellets. This is most notable in America which mainstream culture (mostly financed by bankers vis a vis CIA domestic ops, including but not limited to cultural socio-engineering; starting with Tim Leary, Kurt Cobain, Beavis and Butthead, "Jackass", and now a plethora of other cultural icons, promoting a culture of stupidity.)

In plain English, while the youth is 'stupidifying' their life away, the Elite are slowly eroding your equity through inflation - the hidden tax. **Inflation is caused by oversupply of currency!** The idea that supply and demand drives inflation and deflation is not valid argument in Fiat money system, because the quantity of money in the system M0, M1, M2, M3, MZM, plus currency swaps, derivatives, and countless other financial instruments created in the base currency by the central bank; is an ever increasing base number. In the event this trend reversed, that supply of currency decreased, it would still be a changing number, as determined by central banks. Therefore, traditional economics of supply and demand and the price mechanism, is irrelevant. Monetary policy is the only determination of the value of currency, in a Fiat system. How does this impact average people in America, and in Russia? Every year, you have less money to buy things (whether groceries, property, health care services, etc.)

Lie #2: US Dollars are money

US Dollars and most global major currencies are debt based currencies. Debt is not money, such as Gold is money. New US Dollars are created only through LENDING, if all US Dollar debt was paid off, it would mean there would be no more US Dollars! Even if you believe that US Dollars are money, in any event, because of a constantly expanding money supply, every year you have less and less money, by keeping assets in US Dollars.

Lie #3: Currencies are backed by something

Fiat currencies are backed only by belief, by faith.

Lie #4: Forex is for international investors, and travelers

All of this propaganda is very effective! The Elite have convinced even self-proclaimed 'financial professionals' and the general mass population that Forex is irrelevant unless you are traveling or do international business.

Here's why Forex is relevant today:
Each central bank, whether it be The Fed or the CBR can only create as much domestic currency as it pleases (it cannot create foreign currency). So, if the Fed creates an additional 100 Trillion via QE 4; it can choose to use that currency domestically, or internationally. If it chooses domestically, it will create hyperinflation. So if this is to be avoided, it must use these freshly created USD to buy foreign currency.

How Forex can benefit domestic population of Russia

Russian population is currently being robbed via collapsing Ruble. Since the 'new ruble' was introduced in 1998 at a rate to USD of 6 Rubles to 1 USD (USD/RUB currently around 70) - this is a loss of about 90% for Ruble denominated assets. What value the Ruble lost in 20 years, it took the US Dollar 80 years to lose.

But when Russia defaulted in 1998 and Moscow was infested with economic hitmen from western banks, they had not only a template from America and soon the EU, they had computers and soon the internet, making a new economic way for the new "Elite" of the new Russia to further rob the people, via hyperinflation of the currency. As in America, oligarchs are created quickly and benefit greatly from hyperinflation, as they can do a number of things to benefit from this situation (most simply, investing their assets in non-domestic currency, but countless other examples as well). Possibly, the rapid depreciation of the currency, could have contributed to the wealth of the oligarch class. In any analysis, since Russia has implemented this system of weakening its domestic currency, the oligarch class has grown in step with America's new superclass.

It is understandable why those in financial services do not understand Forex generally. Because high priests of capitalism preach about 'making money' (which is actually illegal, strictly translated, unless you are the US Mint or the Fed). So by participating in Forex, you aren't really growing your portfolio, you are just breaking even, or **NOT losing**. This lateral thinking should be understood well by Russian population considering their advanced math skills. But it is not widely proliferated in mainstream culture (and very ironically, because major Forex companies are based in Russia). Oh - what the business opportunity!

In a very basic example, imagine you have 1 Million Rubles in 1998. You have transferred them to a US bank account bearing a measly 8% interest in USD (we will not count interest in this example) - roughly, $165,000. 2015 comes around and there's a ruble crisis - fortunately your savings are safe and now gaining about 1% at Everbank, and you need money. You transfer your $165,000 USD back to the motherland, for a whopping 11 Million Rubles! It's roughly 1100% return on your investment in the US Dollar - but of course, you didn't really 'make' any money, you just didn't lose. We shouldn't mention that most of this return is tax free due to FASB rules regarding long term forex investments.

If we consider the interest component, the $165,000 would be $399,000 using this basic calculator, in 2015 this would convert to 27 Million rubles! So, we pose the question; where else in Russia could a single individual get a potential tax free return of 2700%+ by doing basically nothing (a few documents, one bank transfer)?

So, by common people participating in Forex, instead of losing 90% of the value of their currency and complaining to empty TV screens about corrupt politicians, they could have instead made 2700%+ tax free.

This very basic example is simply to illustrate the benefits of average people (whether financial professionals or not) to participate in the Forex market - and that it really is a necessity, if you live in a country like Russia or America when you have a central bank with a policy to destroy the currency. Really though, it's only a tax on working people. If you are very poor - it doesn't matter (you work to live, not live to work). If you are very rich, probably you have assets in America, London, or France. This example doesn't count opportunities such as Forex robots, or the ease of investing in a US stock market bubble which could turn the $165,000 USD into much more (although that part wouldn't be tax free).

Of course, the Elite in Russia (via CBR) will try to convince the local sheeple about the evils and risks of Forex, as they fleece the domestic population via the slow death of the hidden tax of hyperinflation. Baa-baa
Forex is especially necessary where the domestic currency is volatile. Russia is a great example because it's not Zimbabwe, not the EU, and Russia is a globally significant dynamic economy.

So what is the American Forex delusion?
A lie can be the withholding of information. In the case of Forex, it's simply 1% of missing important knowledge that prevents a real understanding of what's going on. In the case of America vs. Russia - The Fed, currently is a private central bank, owned by private banks. The CBR, still officially a public institution owned by 'the people.' But, it was the Americans who invented modern finance. It was the Americans who created modern Forex. It was the Americans that pressed Russia to open their markets (most importantly - financial markets!) - which again, is ironic considering

how Wall St. banks financed Lenin, without which financing the Bolshevik revolution would not have been successful.

So who benefits from this system? The Elite, who strip the common people of their assets (but with style). But also, educated people who know how this system works and can exploit it, such as older examples here, here, and here. The Elite - provide a method for profiting from this situation! There are no shackles, no chains - only those which are in our mind! We can set down that bag of bricks handed to us, and free ourselves. It is the paradox of the modern control paradigm; the tool of control can be used as a means to become a controller! It's just a question, a decision, which side of the trade you want to be on.

The good news - it is possible to profit from this situation, and even prosper. This can be achieved only by education followed by action. It is legal, and possible, for any individual in the world to profit in Forex, and to protect their financial assets. Welcome to the club!

2.1 American Ignorance in the land of the World's Reserve Currency

Since the commencement of World War 2, the United States of America has enjoyed the luxury of being the only significant economic power in the world. A number of factors contributed to massive post WW2 growth in the United States:

- Influx of money (meaning, assets with real value) and trained immigrants into the United States
- Assets seized during WW2 that fueled development

- New export markets (Germany, Japan, UK, France, Italy, etc.) with no domestic competition

<u>**Unwire your brain point 42:**</u>

Common thinking: **THE UNITED STATES GIVES AID TO COUNTRIES AND HELPS PEOPLE**

The reality: BANKS, MANY FROM THE UNITED STATES BUT ALSO EUROPE, PROVIDE UNREASONABLE LOANS TO THOSE IN DESPERATE SITUATIONS, WITH THE GOAL OF LATER SEIZING THEIR BUSINESS ASSETS, KEY INFRASTRUCTURE, OR OPENING UP NEW MARKETS

The best Forex example of the post WW2 US dominance is the Marshall Plan. US Dollars literally rebuilt much of Europe, Japan, and other parts of the world. As an added bonus, these local economies relied on the US for products and services that were lacking locally. But it cost the US nothing to create the billions of dollars sent to these foreign nations. The Marshall Plan was enacted by the US Congress, but look from a monetary perspective. The original source of any US Dollars is the Federal Reserve, and during this time we must also consider the US Mint, because there was no 'electronic' money. But there were $100,000 notes, and other instruments. Also remember that when the US Government needs money, it asks uncle Fed. The US Government is the biggest customer of the Fed.

Street polls are the source of much humor; when asking many Americans what currency they use in England their answer "Queens Dollar" or "US Dollar" – it really was true to a large extent post WW2. It would surprise many Americans that Cuba, a long time enemy of the USA, primarily used US Dollars during the trade embargo.

Behind the scenes, the backing of other currencies was the US Dollar. Because the US Dollar was backed by Gold at that time, US Dollars were seen to be as "Good as Gold" and central banks gladly accepted them as a reserve asset. It was the only currency during that time that was perceived to have any value. So after WW2 the world used a financial system based on the US Dollar. This created a Forex void in the United States itself. While the US hailed itself having the most credible and sophisticated financial markets, it lacked any bank that would offer accounts in Foreign Currency.

Today, only Everbank will offer accounts in Euros, Swiss Francs, and Great British Pounds. There are roughly 7,000 banks in the United States[xx]. So it is amazing that only one bank, Everbank, offers products involving foreign currency. Major Banks will only offer the exchange of cash for travelers, charging upwards of 8% per transaction. Class action lawsuits against these banks specifically about this horrendous practice have not lowered these exorbitant fees. Everbank charges a reasonable .5% per Forex transaction. Why other banks do not do this, is because of the history we are describing here. America has become a Forex void – by being the world's banker.

To contrast this, the majority of foreign banks will offer accounts and products in multiple currencies, and even offer hedging products such as options, forwards, and even spot FX trading. FX is a common component of banking outside the United States.

Even top financial professionals in the United States do not understand Forex! All these comments are meant to paint a picture of *WHY* the current global Forex system is the way it is, not to insult or degrade Americans. America has been a world leader in financial markets and innovation. It is for this reason that it is so strange, and so telling, why Forex is so unknown in the country of financial innovation.

Also strange is that historically speaking, America had the most colorful Forex history before the establishment of the Federal Reserve and US Dollar. Before the Civil War, there were a very large amount of currencies operating in the United States of America. Although we do not know exactly how many due to poor documentation of failed currencies, there were somewhere between 8,000 – 10,000 private currencies and state backed currencies. The value of these currencies was determined by the belief in them – "JP Morgan Bank" currency was more valued than the currency minted by the local business. State currencies were often backed by gold & silver. According to the US Constitution, the Federal Government had the right only to create coin money (not paper) [xxi]. Federal Reserve Notes (FRNs) in circulation today, are property of the Federal Reserve. No mention of the US Government. There's a photo of the US Treasury which is very serious looking. They are very well manufactured – they look like certificates – even better than apostille! But they are issued by a private bank which is not part of the US Government. Actually, the US Government is the Fed's biggest client! What a convenient relationship, when Congress needs money, they can ask Uncle Fed, instead of Uncle Sam. It is no wonder why this unholy alliance is stronger than ever.

Unwire your brain point 44: The US Government spends money borrowed from the Federal Reserve – not from tax dollars! The Federal Reserve creates money out of thin air. Your tax dollars, as they say, are mostly going to pay for interest on that borrowed money that bankers create from nothing. From one perspective, the Fed is a big magnetic black hole that sucks legitimate economic activity into its big black nothingness.

There are several simple answers why Forex is so unknown in America. There are many factors:

- The average American has no need to understand Forex. Including financial professionals, they can always deal in US Dollars – so why bother?
- Bankers spend billions of dollars (which they create from nothing) on propaganda campaigns designed to ensure the status quo.
- Americans have become xenophobic. A nation of immigrants, decided to become jingoists. Americans can even be offended by 'foreign' things, and especially 'foreign currency' – *it looks like monopoly money!*

Bankers invest heavily in technologies used to make Americans ignorant, fat, and happy. Without getting technical, it combines biological, chemical, psychological, social, and cultural programming techniques. These techniques have been perfected over a period of 50 years, such that today, it's nearly impossible for any intelligence to escape from the average American. In its most humiliating and disturbing form, The Federal Reserve itself publishes a series of cartoon comic books designed for teaching finance majors and high school students:

The New York Fed has published comics about money and finance for younger readers more interested in cartoons than macroeconomics since the 1950s, according to Edward Steinberg, a retired former Fed employee who authored several of the comic books available online today. From 1993 to 2002, Steinberg directed the communications staff at the Federal Reserve Bank of New York's public information department. In that role, he oversaw a small team of writers and editors that produced the Fed's print publications and educational materials, such as the comic books. Of the five comics Steinberg wrote himself, three were updates of the Fed's longest-running titles, while two, The Story of the Federal Reserve System and The Story of Monetary Policy were new additions to the Fed's extensive comics catalog. [Figure 3 Panels from The Story of Money, written by Edward Steinberg and illustrated by Norman Nodel.]

Distributed free of charge to teachers, the comics were mostly aimed at high school students, whom Steinberg felt weren't learning enough about the economy and personal finance, but some of the more advanced titles, such as The Story of Monetary Policy, have been taught in several college classrooms. Many of the comics are still in distribution today—The Story of Money, which was first published in 1994, has since been revised and reprinted a dozen times in batches of around 250,000 copies[xxii].

These scary depictions come from the Federal Reserve directly and are available for free – they will even pay the shipping. Supposedly designed for school teachers, anyone can order them – even foreigners.

Modern propaganda was invented by Edward Bernays and its use spread in the United States during the same time when the USD became the world's reserve currency. We don't use 'propaganda' because that's bad – now it's 'marketing.' The connection between the Hollywood propaganda machine and Wall St. has been honed down to a science. The promotion globally of the US Dollar as a financial brand, should not be suspect. Of course, any business wants to promote the use of its product. So it should not be surprising that the Federal Reserve wants you to use its only product – US Dollars! But there's so much paradox and irony in FX – their marketing budget – **unlimited!**

Whether intended or not, this marketing campaign had its greatest effect on the domestic population. It is successful overseas – the US Dollar is believed to be around the world 'as good as gold' when in fact it's backed by nothing. But there are doubters. This campaign promoting the US Dollar – it is a major reason why there is no Forex understanding in America. Because 'I only use dollars' – why should I bother to spend a moment of my free time learning about other currencies in the world (especially when there is Football tonight).

Let's use another example to understand why Forex is so lacking in America. Imagine that there is a game of control of the world's economy, and that each central bank tries to promote the use of its currency more than any other. The Fed controls banking functions such as check clearing, ACH payments (Automated Clearing House), Fed Wire payment services, and many others. Also, as the 'lender of last resort' – they support the entire banking system. So to use Euros at your US Bank – you risk being cut off by your only guaranteed support – the Fed. It is in their interest on a banking level, a social & cultural level, and legal level – to promote the only thing they can manufacture without cost on an unlimited basis – US Dollars!

And finally, Forex is not taught at US Universities. The most bizarre example of this is the fact that they teach at leading "Business Schools" interest rate parity theory. According to this theory, we can predict the value of EUR/USD in 6 months by dividing the prevailing interest rates of the two currencies, multiplied by the capital flows in between the two countries. This of course is ridiculous – but the model works with a pre-Nixon shock Forex system of fixed currency rates (or even those trading in a snake or band). Now we call these simply "Forward contracts" and they are just a tool in the Forex hedging toolbox. It is a case that is endemic at Universities in many subjects, they are teaching concepts that are severely outdated.

2.2 Information Arbitrage
Bankers have long profited from information known only to them. One of the most infamous historical accounts is that of the Rothschild agents being able to cross both enemy lines (as they financed both sites) during the battle of Waterloo, receiving advanced information about the victory and thus profiting

greatly from it. Although this account has proven to be either false or greatly exaggerated[xxiii], it serves as a great example of information arbitrage. In this time, there was no internet – no faster communication than pigeon. Yes, pigeons were used for communication during the medieval period in Europe, and a British sport exists "Pigeon Racing" where trained birds will compete who can deliver the message faster [xxiv] . Although Pigeon is slower than internet – it's certainly faster than man or horse, thereby giving anyone using communication Pigeons a huge information advantage. Imagine knowing the battle outcome before other investors!

To prevent information arbitrage in the stock market, or at least to make it on the surface a fair playing field, many rules have been enacted regarding the disclosure of information. As we are led to believe, investors should have all information they need to make decisions about investing. Most critically, is the coveted 'insider information' which is greatly prosecuted and contested. Those with intimate knowledge of a company should not profit from the information unfairly; because they have an advantage over other investors.

There are no insider trading rules pertaining to Forex

Information arbitrage is widespread in Forex. It is questionably ethical but 100% legal. In fact this issue has never been addressed by a serious, qualified professional body such as the US Congress. After 9/11 there were investigations over put options on UAL and other stocks most affected by the event. The names of several institutions who made millions on these options were never made public.   But the Forex implications were never mentioned, and never investigated. Take any Forex chart and plot related terrorist events and you'll see that often, the move in FX **precedes the event!** Sometimes by several hours! Assuming that real terrorists do not have sufficient capital to move FX markets, we can assume that someone in the west, whether a connected individual, intelligence agency, or a bank working with an intelligence agency, had prior knowledge.

Here's another link between the CIA and Wall St. – between intelligence agencies and international banking. The CIA often collects valuable intelligence which can have impacts on markets.   It's often disproved that such information could be used on the NYSE or other US domestic stock exchanges. But no mention of Forex – in any case it would be difficult to account, considering Forex is not traded on a public exchange.   But stocks are traded on public exchanges, so we have a paper trail preceding any significant event:

Although uniformly ignored by the mainstream U.S. media, there is abundant and clear evidence that a number of transactions in financial markets indicated specific (criminal) foreknowledge of the September 11 attacks on the World Trade Center and the Pentagon. In the case of at least one of these trades -- which has left a $2.5 million prize unclaimed -- the firm used to place the "put options" on United Airlines stock was, until 1998, managed by the man who is now in the number three Executive Director position at the Central Intelligence Agency. Until 1997 A.B. "Buzzy" Krongard had been Chairman of the investment bank A.B.

Brown. *A.B. Brown was acquired by Banker's Trust in 1997. Krongard then became, as part of the merger, Vice Chairman of Banker's Trust-AB Brown, one of 20 major U.S. banks named by Senator Carl Levin this year as being connected to money laundering. Krongard's last position at Banker's Trust (BT) was to oversee "private client relations." In this capacity he had direct hands-on relations with some of the wealthiest people in the world in a kind of specialized banking operation that has been identified by the U.S. Senate and other investigators as being closely connected to the laundering of drug money*[xxv].

All of these unusual connections may be circumstantial. But the strong connection between Wall St. and the intelligence community is well known publicly. Even on the public websites of agencies such as CIA, FBI and others, they mention their job is to protect America's 'critical infrastructure' one of which (if not the most important) is the financial markets. But because their activities are secret, we will never know the true extent to which they work with private Wall St. banks on critical deals. We will never know if it is an untold agency policy, or just a rogue agent providing information to his Yale college buddies.

⊙ **"Other information services (including news syndicates, libraries, internet publishing and broadcasting)" (519100)**

Includes things like:

News Syndicates, Libraries and Archives, All Other Information Services, Monetary Authorities - Central Bank

But what is really mind blowing, Turbo Tax 2016 lists business examples for the category "Other Information Services" including news syndicates, libraries, and Central Banks (Monetary Authorities)! Even from the perspective of classification and identification, Forex is an information business, not a financial business. A central bank is a provider of "Other Information Services" - there we have the real definition of what is Money and what is Forex – **Forex is information.** A real Foreign Money exchange, is the exchange of information.

As has been proven in recent Forex cases[xxvi], major Forex dealers exchange information between each other about significant market events, and big client orders. They even colluded to 'manipulate' the Forex market (it's impossible to manipulate the Forex market, unless you are a central bank) to their own favor. Actually what they did was very low trick. They sat on client orders and waited for the market to move against their clients, before offsetting risk. In some cases, they'd try to push the market (price leaning) only slightly with small orders. This is hardly market manipulation, although it's highly unethical, highly unfair, and should be stopped as a market practice.

If the banks have settled this issue for $2 Billion, you can rest assured the profit they made from this activity was 10x or 20x that amount. Also interesting, is that major Forex ECNs (Electronic Communications Networks, or Interbank Forex marketplace) are owned and operated by news agencies, most notably Reuters. When most people think of Reuters, they think of the leading news agency. They don't know that Reuters has an active Forex business, and was until recently one of the top providers of Forex trading to institutions in the world. Reuters is not only a Forex platform, it's a news agency that releases economic data that impacts the markets. It's not a conflict of course, in fact – Reuters offers a service "Ultra Low Latency Economic Indicators and Reuters Macroeconomic

News" effectively allowing their clients to front-run the FX markets, for a fee[xxvii]. They've made a legitimate business out of information arbitrage. Isn't it interesting how the evolution of information arbitrage, starting with trusted house shields "Rothschild" and homing Pigeons, has evolved into High Frequency algorithms run by artificial intelligence software. The markets have become an entity by themselves.

With electronic trading, and now algorithmic trading – the next evolution of the markets will be intelligent trading systems competing against each other for market supremacy. In other words, information arbitrage will always exist but in a different form. The latency of information during the time of the battle of Waterloo was several days. Now, latency arbitrage strategies that were traded in the past 5 years have taken advantage of 10 MS (millisecond) advantages over their counterparties. Now that time is near zero and the market 'knows' everything, the only next logical evolutionary step is intelligence. The cost of developing such machine learning algorithms was prohibitive, and certainly would be more complicated when considering securities or commodities markets; their lack of near infinite liquidity, closing times, and huge amount of rules & order types. But now, the amount of profits that can be achieved in Forex can justify such expenses, especially considering central banks are flooding the FX markets with newly printed currencies of their own denomination. Take it into consideration when understanding Forex or developing your next Forex strategy. Information arbitrage was a cheap trick easily exploited by early market participants, like the oil near the surface which is easy to extract.

Now markets are more efficient, just as the oil is harder to extract from the ground. There's plenty of oil, just no more cheap oil.

3: Forex Regulatory Anomalies

Forex, strictly speaking, is unregulated. Because by definition, "Forex" is the Foreign exchange of one currency into another. Therefore, the only super regulator of Forex would be an international organization such as the United Nations (UN), Bank of International Settlements (BIS), or some would be world government regulator. Another thin nuance of Forex regulation is the fact that the only entities explicitly authorized to trade Forex are banks; banks are regulated by their domestic banking regulators but more importantly, are underwritten by the central bank in their jurisdiction, especially as it pertains to Forex. Central Banks generally do not trade Forex directly, they do so through their member banks. Although, there are many notable exceptions, such as Bank Negara of Malaysia that traded Forex as a wealth diversification strategy, leading to its insolvency in 1994. Banks receive their authority from central banks, who receive their authority from either governments (i.e. the public) or private banks. In the case of private central banks, this creates a supernova regulatory anomaly. Who owns the Federal Reserve is practically irrelevant.

Anyhow, paper ownership is something the Elite dangle in front of the unwashed and unenlightened to lure them to do their bidding.

As any high level tax advisor or multi-generational wealth planner will tell you – having assets in your name is a liability, not equity – from a strategic point of view. Baron families such as Carnegie, Rockefeller, and so on, have long divested their interests into a series of domestic NGOs, Charities, family trusts, and unique entities, that their paper wealth (and thus their liability) is minimized. Therefore, who is the named shareholder of the private Federal Reserve is irrelevant! Officially, the US Federal Reserve is owned by its member banks[xxviii]. The real question is not who owns the Fed, but who receives the trillions of dollars in interest payments, and who receives the trillions of dollars in USD swaps to 'save' the system.

Not all central banks are private. In fact most central banks are 100% public institutions, owned and operated by the government (essentially, by the people). This topic pertains to Forex regulatory anomalies, and why they exist.

In the United States, the retail investing into 'off exchange' Forex contracts is regulated by the CFTC[xxix] (Commodities Futures Trading Commission) through the NFA (National Futures Association), a SRO (Self-Regulatory Organization). This was enacted by the infamous dud-fag act as some traders call it, officially "Dodd–Frank Wall Street Reform and Consumer Protection Act[xxx]

SUMMARY: The Commodity Futures Trading Commission ("Commission" or "CFTC") is adopting a comprehensive regulatory scheme to implement the provisions of the Dodd-Frank Wall Street Reform and Consumer Protection Act of 2010 ("Wall Street Reform Act") 1 and the CFTC Reauthorization Act of 2008 ("CRA") 2 with respect to off exchange transactions in foreign currency with members of the retail public (i.e., "retail forex transactions"). The new regulations and amendments to existing regulations published today establish requirements for, among other things, registration, disclosure, recordkeeping, financial reporting, minimum capital, and other operational standards. DATES: Effective Date: October 18, 2010.[xxxi]

After 22,000 pages of regulation, this act effectively shut down the budding FX industry in the United States. Practically, Dodd-Frank was probably not intended to stifle the Forex industry, or a conspiracy to establish a one world currency or the Amero, as some have theorized. At the heart of Dodd-Frank were derivatives newly created, along with new policies and practices, mostly tied to the housing market. Forex was just the bad step-child of subprime lending. The problem with Forex in the mid-2000's in the United States was simply that because Forex was unregulated, it attracted a vile criminal element. Financial fraud was so rampant during this period, some managers experienced only a 6 month time window in order to trade customer accounts before the institution would go bust. From hundreds of Forex brokers in the United States during the 2005 – 2010 period, after Dodd-Frank, only a small handful remain. The unintended consequence of Dodd-Frank was simply pushing the remaining legitimate Forex players overseas. In parallel to the destruction of the US Forex industry, a massive explosion of non-US Forex business expanded at astounding rates. Meta Trader estimates the number of brokers using their software at 1,500+ as of 2014; so based on this we can estimate the number of retail Forex brokers in the world is near 10,000 (including white labels).

The NFA created a new regulatory category for "Forex" companies, which entail special Forex rules and pay higher fees. The traditional FCM (Futures Commissions Merchant) now can register as an RFED (Retail Foreign Exchange Dealer). The NFA didn't create the regulations, it is only an enforcement agency, and a voluntary one at that. So NFA should not be blamed for Forex related rules. In fact, the NFA and CFTC have uncovered many Forex frauds, some of whom were NFA Members and some not.

3.1 The Golden Years of US Algorithmic Forex – 2003 to 2010

The .com boom had a net positive effect on the concept of retail electronic trading. It popularized the idea that you could do your own investing, and that you could even make a living out of it (although 90% of those who try will fail within 6 months). But the .com boom left many day-traders and would be hobby traders left scratching their heads. During the .com boom in the late 90's – it was easy to make money day-trading. Traders could often randomly pick stocks in the tech sector and make money. Even with the rampant IPO fraud of the time, overall many still grew their accounts consistently – until the .com crash. The market withered for some time until the fateful events of 9/11 which shifted the mood from one of excitement and technology to one of security and war. Heavily armed guards and armored vehicles guarded the entrance to the NYSE. Constant threats and fears persisted that 'terrorists' would attack financial centers 'because they hate freedom.' Excitement turned into fear; many traders went off the grid. In parallel, markets became more and more electronic. It was possible to trade from a remote location or a home office. More and more financial institutions relocated away from WTC (World Trade

Center), the previous hub of Wall St., and into New Jersey and surrounding areas. The trading floor evolved into the data center. Finally, as of this writing, all physical exchanges have gone electronic. While the NYSE maintains a 'trading floor' at the original location, it serves only as a fancy office, where specialists mull around looking at handheld devices.

During this time, traders (both retail and institutional) were searching for new ways to trade, and new markets to trade. Also – there was much talk about the value of the US Dollar in respect to global events - and there was Forex! It was a natural introduction to the Forex market. What attracted many traders to Forex as a market were the features of the market itself, not the fact that it was "Forex." Forex provides traders:

- Near infinite liquidity (from the perspective of the individual trader)
- Always open – only closed on Saturdays
- Mathematically simple market, compared to other markets
- Ability to trade algorithms on a growing number of retail platforms, starting with Tradestation
- Huge leverage, up to 500:1 compared to the measly 2:1 or 4:1 in stocks, and a little more in futures.
- A large number of currency pairs to trade

Also in parallel during this time was the development of many online Forex platforms, which made it possible to open an account with little risk. At Oanda it was possible to open an account for a dollar – a single US dollar. Since trading was mostly electronic, it was only fitting that algorithmic trading of Forex grew in popularity. Forex trading can be brutal even for the experienced bank trader. One famous tale of a Forex trader from a bank fell down a manhole in NYC walking back from lunch. It's not for the faint of heart. Algorithms on the other hand – are perfect for Forex! The Russian company MetaQuotes was in the right place at the right time – they offered a Microsoft Windows product "Meta Trader" to Forex brokers that enabled customers to develop algorithms in a sandbox environment, while offering the Forex dealers a plethora of sliders, buttons, alarms, and algorithms such as the infamous "Virtual Dealer" to literally screw the customer out of their profits. Meta Trader's popularity peaked with version 4, or MT4 – the perfect environment for the battle of the bots. It was customer against the institution, advantage institution. Because of the Forex regulatory anomaly during this time, many institutions used this popular MT4 platform to perpetrate their frauds. In extreme cases, millions in customer money was not even traded in the real Forex market – live customer accounts were in 'demo' mode, meaning that what they thought were Forex trades entering the interbank market, were actually demo trades or 'paper trading' as it's known in the stock industry.

But also, customers exploited known flaws in the MT4 system to take advantage of the brokers who were in many cases, not tech savvy. In one of the most interesting cases, a strategy was developed such that it would make constant quote requests faster than the client terminal would allow, and place a trade in the terminal that was better than the real market price. This practice was easily stopped by Meta Quotes via a software update, but before the update many customers made a lot of money using this method. Another popular exploit, later used by institutional traders 'latency arbitrage' would seek price discrepancies in milliseconds in between 2 MT4 brokers and capture the difference. In this case it was nearly impossible for the broker to prove that customers were doing this.

Independent of this cat and mouse game, there were few stable Forex brokerages during this time. It was fraud season in the new Forex market, started very dramatically with the Refco bankruptcy. A volume of books could be dedicated to the frauds of this time, each with its own peculiarities. Some frauds have yet to be uncovered. But many companies survived and now flourish, such as ATC Brokers, who has even opened a licensed Forex brokerage in London with the FCA, as well as operating a US based independent Introducing Broker.

3.2 Unique Frauds

In 2014 the United States senate published a report outlining potentially fraudulent activities of Wall St.'s 3 largest banks; Goldman, JP, and Morgan[xxxii]. In plain English, Wall St. has invested in physical commodity infrastructure, operates commodity businesses, trades in the commodity markets, and provides cheap financing to do so (via the Fed). This situation is a Monopolist's dream; they literally control the entire system from start to finish, even transportation and logistics.

In 2010, Goldman Sachs purchased a Detroit company that is responsible for storing most of the exchange-traded aluminum in the United States. At the same time Goldman ramped up its trading in aluminum to a peak of $3 billion in 2012. The report asserts that Goldman used unorthodox measures raise the prices. The New York Times had referred to this as the "merry-go-round of metal," a description the Senate subcommittee also used.

...Federal Reserve rules mandate that bank holding companies cannot hold physical commodity assets that exceed 5 percent of their capital. But the report says that JPMorgan Chase held physical commodities assets in 2012 that were equivalent to 12 percent of a measure of the bank's capital. The bank justified this by assigning those commodities to its bank, rather than the bank holding company.

It seems that banking regulation has come down to splitting hairs, and these banks have very sharp razors. This fraud, which amounts to complete market manipulation, is legal and within regulatory guidelines. Is it the case, that business is always just a little smarter than regulations? What are implications for Forex, a completely unregulated market? While this fraud is not about Forex, it is these banks who control the Forex market – what implications does it have for their Forex operations?

Many frauds have used Forex as a marketing tool only, and really have nothing at all to do with Forex. The most well-crafted and mysterious of all is probably "Secure Investment" operated online from secureinvestment.com, who took probably about $1 Billion from victims [xxxiii]. The perpetrators are still at large; one day the site vanished without a trace.

Secure Investment had paid actors to provide testimonials about the quality of their service. Customer support always replied promptly and professionally, and even allowed customers to withdraw small funds. They used a spider web of shells in Belize, Panama, Hong Kong, Australia, and in other jurisdictions. They often changed their bank accounts, and always provided customers with a reasonable response. There was absolutely no suspicion about them until they day they disappeared with $1 Billion in victim funds. They provided customers with an online accounts system that showed Forex trades and their accounts growing. But in reality, this company was just taking customer money and keeping it for themselves.

Secure crafted a tangled financial web to harvest and hide investor money by setting up companies with different names incorporated in Belize, the British Virgin Islands and the U.K. Secure asked clients in e-mails to wire money to bank accounts held by those firms. By using related companies, Secure obscured the paper trail of investor funds that would end up with the firm. The only public evidence that authorities have looked into Secure Investment comes from Panama. In July 2013, the website of Panama's securities regulator, SMV, warned that the company wasn't licensed or authorized to trade currencies.
The regulator also said Secure Investment listed a false Panama City address as its headquarters. The office addresses that Secure's website listed in Hong Kong, London and Sydney were also phony. All of those were at sites run by international office leasing company Regus Plc. London-based spokesman Andrew Brown researched his company's records and found that Secure never used any of those locations.

Forex is so widely misunderstood, it has provided criminals and fraudsters with the perfect story to swindle unsuspecting victims out of their hard earned money. But these Ponzi schemes and frauds really have nothing to do with Forex. Taking a look at the recent Forex Settlements against the big Forex banks, such fraud was not limited to a retail level; although the institutional fraud was of a different nature. But in both cases, those with slightly greater Forex knowledge take advantage of those with slightly less. By the end of this book, you can learn to detect "Forex Fraud" better than any financial police, auditor, regulator, or investigator.

3.3 Forex Tax Havens

There are an innumerable number of Forex rules that make the use of Forex itself a virtual tax haven. For example, according to the IRS, for tax purposes, owning a foreign currency is looked at as debt!

> *Section 988.--Treatment of Certain Foreign Currency Transactions*
>
> *An instrument that requires payments to be made in a foreign currency (that is, nonfunctional currency) can be debt for U.S. federal income tax purposes. Click here to view / download IRS PDF Section 988.--Treatment of Certain Foreign Currency Transactions*
>
> *Original source from irs.gov: https://www.irs.gov/pub/irs-drop/rr-08-1.pdf*

We hear a lot in the news about US corporations taking advantage of tax loopholes, by operating foreign corporations in places such as Luxembourg, the Bahamas, and others. But the Forex element – the most important word – is left out of this discussion! Many of these tax reductions are based on Forex rules, not only because funds are in another country. In other words, there is confusion about the domicile of money. According to the above IRS rule, funds kept within the borders of the United States, at a bank that offered a non-USD account such as Everbank – would be considered debt. This could be a billion dollar financial strategy for the CFO of a major corporation. But instead of utilizing Forex rules to grow business, save money, and create jobs – they do the opposite. They use Forex as an excuse for being bad, untrained financial planners. Just google 'corporate earnings currency headwinds' or 'currency headwinds' to read a number of articles that justify bad earnings because of Forex. There are hundreds of explicit examples of the opposite, such as when Intel Corporation made more money from Forex than selling processors (Millman, 1995). Japanese car manufacturers such as Toyota who have their own banks, often capitalize on Forex trends to grow their business. In fact, some economies rely on this to compete in world markets. To put this in practical perspective for a moment, that it isn't thought this is some sort of 'magic' – let's take the following example.

A company like McDonald's (MCD) has regular income in foreign currency which is relatively fixed. They know they will have X Million revenue in Russian Ruble because they operate 400+ stores in Russia. Normally they convert Ruble to USD quarterly for their earnings. What they could do, is sell covered calls to buy Ruble (which they have, naturally). In the case these sold options expire in the money, they simply would provide the Rubles to the purchaser of the option, and gain nothing (other than disposing of their Ruble position). But if the options expire out of the money, MCD has just created money for nothing; an income stream based on the fact that they operate in Russia! Yes, there are corporations who do this, and successfully – such as noted by Millman in his book "Vandal's Crown." This profit they would make from this activity – largely tax free! It's because of Forex accounting & hedging rules.   McDonald's is not speculating in the Forex market, they are hedging their own Forex risk by selling covered calls (the Forex equivalent).

McDonald's is an interesting Forex example, because it's an All-American company that sells an All-American product: Hamburgers. But also, McDonald's is faced every quarter with the same "Currency Headwinds" that can materially change their financials.   Also interesting, McDonald's is the namesake of one of the best Forex economic indicators: The Big Mac Index.[xxxiv] *The **Big Mac Index** is published by The Economist as an informal way of measuring the purchasing power parity (PPP) between two currencies and provides a test of the extent to which market exchange rates result in goods costing the same in different countries. **It "seeks to make exchange-rate theory a bit more digestible".** The Big Mac PPP exchange rate between two countries is obtained by dividing the price of a Big Mac in one country (in its currency) by the price of a Big Mac in another country (in its currency). This value is* then compared with the actual exchange rate; if it is lower, then the first currency is under-valued (according to PPP theory) compared with the second, and conversely, if it is higher, then the first currency is over-valued. For example, using figures in July 2008:

1. the price of a Big Mac was $3.57 in the United States (varies by store)
2. the price of a Big Mac was £2.29 in the United Kingdom (varies by region)
3. the implied purchasing power parity was $1.56 to £1, that is $3.57/£2.29 = 1.56
4. this compares with an actual exchange rate of $2.00 to £1 at the time
5. (2.00-1.56)/1.56 = 28%
6. the pound was thus overvalued against the dollar by 28%

The Eurozone is mixed, as prices differ widely in the EU area. As of April 2009, the Big Mac is trading in Germany at €2.99, which translates into US$3.96, which would imply that the euro is slightly trading above the PPP, with the difference being 10.9%.

THE BIG MAC INDEX
How many burgers you get for $50 USD?

Rank	Country	Price		Rank	Country	Price
30	India*	$1.62		23	Ukraine	$2.11
					Hong Kong	$2.12
21	Malaysia	$2.34		20	China	$2.44
					South Africa	$2.45
					Indonesia	$2.46
					Thailand	$2.46
					Taiwan	$2.5
19	Russia	$2.55		18	Saudi Arabia	$2.67
	Sri Lanka	$2.55			Philippines	$2.68
	Egypt	$2.57			Mexico	$2.7
	Poland	$2.58				
	Hungary	$2.63				
17	Lithuania	$2.87		16	Latvia	$3.0
	Pakistan	$2.89				
15	South Korea	$3.19		14	Czech Rep.	$3.45
	UAE	$3.27			Turkey	$3.54
13	Peru	$3.71		12	Costa Rica	$4.02
	Singapore	$3.75			Chile	$4.05
	Britain	$3.82			New Zealand	$4.05
					Israel	$4.13
					Japan	$4.16
11	USA	$4.2		10	Canada	$4.63
	Euro area	$4.43			Uruguay	$4.63
	Colombia	$4.54			Argentina	$4.64
					Australia	$4.94
9	Denmark	$5.37		8	Brazil	$5.68
					Sweden	$5.91
7	Norway	$6.79				
	Switzerland	$6.81				

Source: The Economist (Jan 2012)
* Chicken burger

The reason we know so little about Forex is the same as many things; we hear about the frauds, the problems, the lack of understanding. We don't hear about the Swiss hedge fund making millions per week in risk free profits trading latency arbitrage, or the corporations who make billions in Forex. Money Center banks reap huge profits in Forex, but because of accounting standards, often the amount and degree to which they profit in Forex can be misleading, especially as published on their publicly available financial statements. Unless there is a fraud or investigation, this data remains private and not possible to study. But there are sufficient examples to make the statement that Forex is a huge profit center with easily manageable risk!

Many Forex tax havens exist, simply look at the IRS rules. What if all the money in a portfolio is deployed using 100% available margin in a complex trade which is nearly 100% hedged? It's a complex derivative, which cannot be taxed. Open positions cannot be taxed until they are closed. Being long & short the market in any currency is the ideal tax haven.

But such examples will never be discussed because they don't even show up on balance sheets. Of course they are there – if you know what to look for. Forex is much deeper than a line item "Forex P/L" but accounting standards do not provide sufficient rules to explain them. To decide about Forex tax treatment depends more on the method, rather than the concept. For example, opening an account at a retail Forex broker and having a profit, is no different than trading stocks – it is a capital gain. But sending US Dollars to a European bank, is a completely different tax situation. Use of Forex derivatives such as options, can be business expenses outright (similar to insurance). So the ways in which Forex is used, will determine the tax benefit or liability.

4: Forex Law & USD regulation

Using the US Dollar in any jurisdiction can make you subject to US Law. By touching that green dollar bill, you are engaging in a legal contract with the Federal Reserve Bank and with the US Government; at least that is the implication. The Department of Justice (DOJ) and other agencies will of course use any hook to prosecute foreign nationals. "Wire fraud" being a catch all for any illegal activity carried over 'wire' communication which is technically speaking all communications, which at some point will be transmitted through US internet cables. This may sound far reaching to even those in the legal field who are knowledgeable about such matters. Even in the recent case *Licci* v. *Lebanese Canadian Bank, SAL* (N.Y. Nov. 20, 2012) [xxxv] it was correspondent accounts in the state of New York at a New York bank, which established venue; not the fact that US Dollars were used.

Then why do some foreign hedge funds not use the US Dollar by purpose, in order to avoid any implications in such matters? Yes, it's possible to trade Forex without the US Dollar. Most foreign brokers offer non-USD base accounts, such as EUR, JPY, GBP, CHF, CAD, and others.

From a report by White & Case:

...This broad jurisdiction can greatly expand the reach of the US money laundering statutes. For example, US corporations and individuals potentially may be prosecuted for money laundering offenses involving financial transactions that occur wholly outside the

United States. US courts have held that the financial transaction requirement is satisfied for a wholly foreign transaction if the defendant's conduct "affected" foreign commerce with the US — such as in antitrust matters. **Virtually every dollar-denominated transaction potentially implicates US commerce with other nations. ...** *"Transit of money through the United States on the way from one non-US location to another non-US location may be enough to create US criminal jurisdiction."*

It seems that the Forex system has much deeper implications into how the world works than appears on the surface! Enforcing these laws in other countries is the topic for another book, but we all know the deep rooted connection between the Military and Wall St. It is even taught in all economics classes in the US that the Military is good for business, that every $1 invested in the Military = $2 in economic output (which is a logical fallacy, this is an organization that is trained to destroy infrastructure and kill people – hardly an economic beneficial activity). But the rise of the US Dollar as a world reserve currency as linked to US Military supremacy, does not need to be studied in great detail. When Nixon created the modern Forex system, in parallel he created the Petro Dollar system, with many layers of support for the US Dollar and Oil from the Middle East whenever the US needed it.

The untold policy of "Use the US Dollar or we bomb you" is a two way street. On the one hand – client nations can enjoy not only protection from the greatest military power in the world, but they can have access to the latest military technology for themselves. Also, they are free to invest in US capital markets, buy

US treasuries, and US real estate (but not ports and other key assets!). On the other hand, if they don't use this well-oiled machine (pun intended) – they can be subject to toppling, assassination, or worse. Interesting examples include but are not limited to Iraq, Libya, and recently Ukraine.

Nixon was an unintended genius in this regard – the Nixon administration understood nothing about global finance. This is in the opinion of Henry Kissinger, advisor to Nixon:

*Secretary Kissinger: But if they ask what they're doing— let me just say **economics is not my forte**. But my understanding of this proposal would be that they—by opening it up to other countries, they're in effect putting gold back into the system at a higher price.*
Mr. Enders: Correct.
Secretary Kissinger: Now, that's what we have consistently opposed.
Mr. Enders: Yes, we have. You have convertibility if they—
Secretary Kissinger: Yes.
Mr. Enders: Both parties have to agree to this. But it slides towards and would result, within two or three years, in putting gold back into the centerpiece of the system—one. Two—at a much higher price. Three—at a price that could be determined by a few central bankers in deals among themselves.
*So, in effect, I think what you've got here is you've got **a small group of bankers getting together to obtain a money printing machine for themselves**. They would determine the value of their reserves in a very small group.*
There are two things wrong with this.

Secretary Kissinger: And we would be on the outside.
Mr. Enders: We could join this too, but there are only very few countries in the world that hold large amounts of gold—United States and Continentals being most of them. The LDC's and most of the other countries—to include Japan—have relatively small amounts of gold. So it would be highly inflationary, on the one hand— and, on the other hand, a very inequitable means of increasing reserves.
Secretary Kissinger: Why did the Germans agree to it?
Mr. Enders: The Germans agreed to it, we've been told, on the basis that it would be discussed with the United States—conditional on United States approval.

Secretary Kissinger: They would be penalized for having held dollars. [xxxvi]

These transcripts were released by the Department of State only several years ago – and have huge implications to understanding Forex. It was US President Richard Nixon, and his advisors, who created the free floating electronic exchange system that we have today. The motives of Nixon are not as important as the net effect; the US Dollar needed to from then on be supported by the US Military.

The dollar was no longer backed by Gold, so it needed to be backed by bombs. And it is so.

This can be a reason why Forex is not taught in US universities. It also explains why such draconian regulations are being implemented.

The regulatory power of the Federal Reserve Bank of New York has shifted to a committee in Washington *established in a previously undisclosed paper written in 2010, the Wall Street Journal reported on Thursday. The change, which the newspaper said had been enacted slowly during the past five years, moves the center of banking oversight to Washington and the Large Institution Supervision Coordinating Committee, headed by Fed Governor Daniel Tarullo." It was obvious that a lot in the U.S. regulatory system had not worked particularly well before the crisis," Tarullo told the Journal. "It was equally obvious that there was going to need to be a rethink and reorganization." The Journal cited Washington officials as saying that centralized regulatory authority in Washington will give a broader, more even-handed approach to oversight. The New York Fed had dominated bank regulation but was denied requests for more representatives on the new committee. **"This reserve bank doesn't breathe any more without asking Washington if it can inhale or exhale,"** said one person prominent in the banking community told the newspaper.[xxxvii]*

Like in central banking, ownership is irrelevant when you can control. In other words, the ability to enforce US law physically, is more significant than any legal argument. Since the Nixon shock and the end of the Vietnam War, the US Military has been on an aggressive worldwide campaign tour promoting the use of the US Dollar, even at gunpoint. By consolidating Forex brokers domestically, in the event of a run on the dollar (such as happened in 2008), a 'buy only' mode could be enforced electronically. Capital controls, now already in place, would be extended. It could be impossible to wire US Dollars overseas, or forbidden to transfer them to another currency, should the need arise.

If this sounds far-fetched, remember Executive Order 6102[xxxviii], signed on April 5, 1933, by President Franklin D. Roosevelt "forbidding the Hoarding of gold coin, gold bullion, and gold certificates within the continental United States". The effect of the order, in conjunction with the statute under which it was issued, was to criminalize the possession of monetary gold by any individual, partnership, association or corporation.

How difficult would it be, if the US Dollar started to collapse, for a US President to issue a 'sell freeze' making it illegal, such as a violation of the Patriot Act, to sell US Dollars?   More practically, because the Federal Reserve controls the supply of US Dollars, and because there are only a small handful of Forex companies which will exchange US Dollars for foreign currency, it would be easy to make it impossible to exchange your US Dollars for foreign currency.

Capital Controls have had a soft introduction via FATCA legislation passed in 2010. Foreign banks are now required to hold 30% of foreign outflows from Americans[xxxix]. Failure to comply with FATCA on the banks' end brings the wrath of the IRS (and what else?).   Switzerland was made an example of, probably to show other countries that if the US can strong-arm Switzerland, anyone is touchable. Protecting the US Dollar is a contact sport! And there's no class action rules in Switzerland protecting Swiss Banks from their birthright called 'banking privacy.' Swiss bankers violated their own laws and their 1,000 years of banking culture at the mere hint that the US would do something to them.

Commonly it's thought this exercise in Switzerland was about uncovering billions in untaxed money kept hidden there by the American Nuevo-Elite. Of course on the surface this is true- as the real money power in America keeps their assets in domestic tax havens on US soil and is a little more creative than using 'Swiss Privacy' to hide assets from the IRS. But imagine this from a Forex perspective. Many of those assets in Switzerland were not in US Dollars – they were in Swiss Francs (CHF), Euros, and other non-USD assets. They were not in the United States itself. In the event of a dollar collapse, what assets these Elites had in Switzerland would have been relatively safe. Certainly they would not be wiped out. Now, they are forced to be on the same sinking ship – inside the US Dollar on US soil.

In parallel to the IRS attacking the concept of Swiss Banking which had established itself as an international brand & institution, the Swiss National Bank intervened in the Swiss Franc for the first time (in 2011) and now continues to manipulate their currency according to the needs and wants from their new US friends. Ask any Forex analyst or look at a CHF chart post 2008 – the Swiss Franc was seen as the only currency which was of legitimate investment value. This started during the post 9/11 market concerns about the value of the US Dollar, and was exacerbated by the 2008 credit crisis. The CHF was 40% backed by gold, and because of the culture of banking privacy, legal protection, and just plain old fashioned fiduciary honor – global investors saw the Swiss Franc as the only currency to keep their money in for the long term. Look at this USD/CHF monthly chart, which shows the USD decline from 1.832750 to below .77540.

Not counting interest, investors who kept their money in CHF during this period, not only received banking privacy, they enjoyed a plus 100% return on their money! Find a chart such as above, and you can bet that the situation is being monitored by US intelligence agencies; which will eventually lead to an 'intervention.' What a coincidence, just at the peak of this chart, the CIA has access to Swiss Bank account transactions:

The Swiss government has remained quiet on the issue, but data protection experts and lawyers are concerned by Friday's revelations in the New York Times. US Treasury Secretary John Snow defended the secret program, carried out by the CIA and the Treasury, calling it "government at its best" and a valuable aid for fighting terrorism. Snow confirmed that since just after the attacks on September 11 2001, the Treasury had been tapping into records of the Belgium-based Society for Worldwide Interbank

Financial Telecommunication (Swift) for evidence of potential activity by terror groups.[xl]

Although no terrorists were ever found through this program, it was convenient that CIA & Treasury had access to these records to assist the IRS in retrieving information on Americans who had accounts there (who during this period achieved a 100% + return on their non-USD accounts).

The full details of what happened during this period, through this program or programs, will never be known. But we know the end result. The only remaining legitimate investment grade currency in the world, the Swiss Franc or CHF, was destroyed. More investors seeking to protect themselves from the collapsing US Dollar, were heavily taxed and penalized. Swiss National Bank chief was humiliated in a scandal, and resigned[xli]. The value of the Swiss Franc has since plummeted, and the US Dollar is stronger than ever.   And there remains no legitimate alternative to US Dollar Hegemony.

4.1 The Forex Legal Anomaly
Forex is traded in between banks, in between countries. As there is no Forex marketplace, no Forex exchange, there is no Forex regulation or law specific to Forex itself. Each currency has its own laws & regulations that pertain to that currency only. As we've described about the US Dollar, some try to extend these laws to the far reaches of planet Earth, by use of their currency. Normally, US Law applies only in the jurisdiction of the United States, and 'sort of' territories like Puerto Rico.   But lawyers and US Government officials have tried to stretch that

boundary to the US Dollar itself, even if it is used in another country. If you are in the US embassy in Russia, you are on US soil – an issue established by centuries of international disputes, diplomacy, protocol, and precedent. It is the case with any embassy; the embassy is a small part of jurisdiction in the host country. The US has tried to extend this by claiming that by using US Dollars, which are property of a US entity the Federal Reserve, it establishes a commercial contract with jurisdiction in the United States.

The US is used as an example here because it is the most aggressive of such policies. But even with this aggressive policy, it cannot project jurisdiction over Forex, no matter how powerful. Some rules of other currencies are different. The Russian Ruble only trades during certain market hours.

The only potential regulator for Forex would be an international entity such as the United Nations, the World Bank, or the Bank of International Settlements (BIS). Currently the BIS provides guidance for central banks regarding Forex. Statistics that we know about Forex, such as the size of the market, volumes traded, and other statistics, come from BIS surveys. Although the BIS has no authority over other central banks, and there are no laws and rules explicitly allowing the BIS this authority, most central banks participate because practically, there's no other official guidance regarding Foreign Exchange. Switzerland has always been a financial world leader, especially regarding international issues of trust. As we now know that the only real currency backing in the world is TRUST – the Swiss banking tradition goes a long way to encourage use of the BIS and its rules and systems. The BIS is sort of the United Nations of banking.   From the BIS website[xlii]:

Established on 17 May 1930, the Bank for International Settlements (BIS) is the world's oldest international financial organization. The BIS has 60 member central banks, representing countries from around the world that together make up about 95% of world GDP. The head office is in Basel, Switzerland and there are two representative offices: in the Hong Kong Special Administrative Region of the People's Republic of China and in Mexico City. The mission of the BIS is to serve central banks in their pursuit of monetary and financial stability, to foster international cooperation in those areas and to act as a bank for central banks.

In broad outline, the BIS pursues its mission by:
- *Fostering discussion and facilitating collaboration among central banks;*
- *Supporting dialogue with other authorities that are responsible for promoting financial stability;*
- *Carrying out research and policy analysis on issues of relevance for monetary and financial stability;*
- *Acting as a prime counterparty for central banks in their financial transactions; and*
- *Serving as an agent or trustee in connection with international financial operations.*

This unique bank provides much suspicion among researchers who believe the global Elite are involved in a conspiracy to form a one world government. It's because the BIS has no explicit international authority; central banks join and participate by choice. There are almost no infractions or dissent among members.

Interesting to the Forex Paradox we describe from different parallel perspectives in this book, the BIS was formed by The Hague, the international court used to prosecute Nazis and other German officials after World War 2. The creation and rise to power of the BIS coincided identically, step by step, with the rise in power of the USD as a global reserve currency, and with the US as the dominant military power.

While the BIS is not a regulator per se, whenever there is market turmoil, BIS has something to say. The BIS was critical to the forming and operation of the Bretton Woods agreement, sponsored by the United Nations[xliii]:

> Jul 1944   The United Nations Conference in Bretton Woods agrees to the creation of the International Monetary Fund (IMF) and the World Bank; it also adopts Resolution V calling for the liquidation of the BIS at "the earliest possible moment".

Real Forex Law – as a superset of domestic law – is a complete anomaly.   Various international organizations setup during this time, which are the primary support systems for modern Forex, were established by 'goodwill' only. Always with the backing of the United States and usually hosted by the United States (such as the United Nations in New York, and Bretton Woods meeting in New Hampshire. The Forex Legal void is supported financially, politically, legally, and militarily by the United States. So it's not surprising that the majority of central banks use the US Dollar as their primary foreign reserve currency (they also use Gold and a basket of other foreign currencies.)

The real question about Forex law is in parallel to the question: Does such a thing exist "International Law?" The only significant functional international organizations are those connected to Forex, the BIS, the World Bank, the United Nations, and the IMF. Smaller, less powerful organizations such as the Permanent Court of Arbitration (established in 1899) have limited international authority[xliv].

Eurodollars vs. EUR/USD or Euro/US Dollar

This confusion is a good example of the high amount of Forex confusion in the world. Eurodollars is a term used to describe US Dollars traded overseas – that is, outside the borders and jurisdiction of the United States. EUR/USD is a currency pair, where the Euro is the base pair, traded against the US Dollar. When you see a quote of EUR/USD 1.20 – it means that 1 Euro = $1.20 US Dollars.

Eurodollars are time deposits denominated in U.S. dollars at banks outside the United States, and thus are not under the jurisdiction of the Federal Reserve. Consequently, such deposits are subject to much less regulation than similar deposits within the U.S.. The term was originally coined for U.S. dollars in European banks, but it expanded over the years to its present definition—a U.S. dollar-denominated deposit in Tokyo or Beijing would be likewise deemed a Eurodollar deposit. There is no connection with the eurocurrency or the eurozone. More generally, the euro- prefix can be used to indicate any currency held in a country where it is not the official currency: for example, Euroyen or even Euroeuro[xlv].

Euros, held outside of Europe, are called "Euroeuros." And people wonder why Forex is not understood!

Forex will always be in a legal void, unless there is a one world government and one world currency, which is not likely in the next 100 years. At the slow pace China tries to adapt to western financial standards, it looks like it will be several dynasties before the Yuan can really compete as a world reserve currency.

But at the end of the day, it's how Forex operates that's important. We can analyze and understand Forex better, by looking at its operational parts, rather than its legal structure or lack thereof. But it's good to know, that in Forex – no law applies! Only agreed principles of trade. Forex supersedes nation states, politics, and even religion. It's the only market that runs the global economy with no bias. **In Forex, all money is green.**

4.2 Forex in the courts

At the end of the day, it's courts that decide what's what in our economic system. Although banks have the authority to create money out of nothing, they cannot violate the law. Banks found engaged in illegal activities will be closed and reprimanded.

But what about gray areas? Forex has been shaping the new paradigm of global trade, and in law this is no exception.

Recent Forex cases involving the world's largest banks have exposed 'what really goes on' inside of an FX dealing room. From one perspective, this is the real

Forex. From another, **these dealers are just viruses who have infected the best host in the world; Forex.**

WM Reuters

The WM Reuters case can be one of the most bizarre in modern business. According to the details of the case, injured investors sued the involved banks because they 'manipulated' the Forex market and the WM/Reuters Rates. This caused government investigations into the issue which is ongoing.

The **forex scandal** *(also known as the* **forex probe***) is a financial scandal that involves the revelation, and subsequent investigation, that banks* <u>colluded</u> *for at least a decade to manipulate* <u>exchange rates</u> *for their own financial gain. Market regulators in Asia, Switzerland, the United Kingdom, and the United States began to investigate the $5.3 trillion-a-day* <u>foreign exchange market</u> *(forex) after* <u>Bloomberg News</u> *reported in June 2013 that currency dealers said they had been* <u>front-running</u> *client orders and rigging the foreign exchange benchmark WM/Reuters rates by colluding with counterparts and pushing through trades before and during the 60-second windows when the benchmark rates are set. The behavior occurred daily in the spot foreign-exchange market and went on for at least a decade according to currency traders. At the center of the investigation are the transcripts of electronic* <u>chatrooms</u> *in which senior currency traders discussed with their competitors at other banks the types and volume of the trades they planned to place. The electronic chatrooms had names such as "The Cartel", "The Bandits' Club", "One Team, One Dream" and "The Mafia".[4][5][6] The discussions in the chatrooms were interspersed with* jokes about manipulating the forex market and repeated references to alcohol, drugs, and women.[7] Regulators are particularly focusing in on one small exclusive chatroom which was variously called The Cartel or The Mafia. The chatroom was used by some of the most influential traders in London and membership in the chatroom was highly sought after. Among The Cartel's members were Richard Usher, a former Royal Bank of Scotland (RBS) senior trader who went to JPMorgan as head of spot foreign exchange trading in 2010, Rohan Ramchandani, Citigroup's head of European spot trading, Matt Gardiner, who joined Standard Chartered after working at UBS and Barclays, and Chris Ashton, head of voice spot trading at Barclays. Two of these senior traders, Richard Usher and Rohan Ramchandani, are members of the 13-member Bank of England Joint Standing Committee's chief dealers group.

At least 15 banks including Barclays, HSBC, and Goldman Sachs disclosed investigations by regulators. Barclays, Citigroup, and JPMorgan Chase all suspended or placed on leave senior currency traders. Deutsche Bank, continental Europe's largest lender, was also cooperating with requests for information from regulators. Barclays, Citigroup, Deutsche Bank, HSBC, JPMorgan Chase, Lloyds, RBS, Standard Chartered, UBS and the Bank of England as of June 2014 had suspended, placed on leave, or fired some 40 forex employees. Citigroup had also fired its head of European spot foreign exchange trading, Rohan Ramchandani. Reuters reported hundreds of traders around the world could be implicated in the scandal[xlvi].

The details of this case are absurd. First, **it is impossible to manipulate the Forex market!** If it was possible for a number of banks or dealers to manipulate the Forex market, they wouldn't need any clients, and they would all have Trillions in USD profits. What they are accused of in plain terms is cheating clients, or in the words of a Barclays employee directly "**If you ain't cheating, you ain't trying.**[xlvii]" Cheating clients is bad, cheating clients is wrong, but it's not market manipulation.

Second, it is impossible to manipulate the WM/Reuters rate because it's a snapshot of a mathematical average. Dealers allegedly manipulated the rates by actually buying and selling foreign currency which thus affected the price. They were able to 'nudge' the price a little higher or lower. But they did this by becoming market participants themselves, not by some arbitrary manipulation, such as happens on a retail level. Retail dealers don't manipulate the market they ARE the market – they tell customers what the price is and what you can trade at. In the case of WM/Reuters, dealers exchanged information about client orders which was unfair and not honorable. Dealers should always have a high degree of commercial honor, according to regulations, and also because they have a fiduciary duty to clients. Clients are trusting them with their funds, and they abused that trust.

Third, these clients should not have been trading WM/Reuters rates. In a world of razor thin spreads and near zero latency, even a retail trader can be almost guaranteed the best market price even in volatile conditions. Why these dinosaurs were using

WM/Reuters to trade should also be under investigation. Imagine trading any market and giving your counterparty full information to trade against you – such as 'I'd like to buy 100 Million Euro at exactly 4pm, at any price" – this creates a situation where dealers could be compromised, corrupted, and finally degraded to the reality of the human condition, overpowered by their small reptilian brains they reverted to all they know how to do: petty theft. Call it what you will, what these dealers did was no more pathetic and petty than an older child bullying a smaller child out of his lunch money on the playground. The dealers have the largest banks in the world behind them, including teams of the world's best lawyers, huge salaries, superior financial knowledge, and they reverted to petty theft? It is shameful, but as they say "The opportunity creates the thief."

Anyone who plays in the markets which are largely based on information arbitrage, by immediately telling the counterparty what they will do several hours from now, is like having a 'kick me' sign on your back. For this reason, many serious traders don't use stop losses. As an old adage says, "If you place a stop order it will likely get triggered," referring to the practices of 'stop hunting' by dealers. Since dealers can see an aggregate of all customer positions, dealers will often push the price up and down to trigger massive stops. WM/Reuters is the surface on an ocean of Forex fraud and manipulation. The reason for this is because the "Forex" market doesn't exist per se, it only exists in the interbank market, and only exists based on what your counterparty tells you. On a high institutional, interbank API level, it's pretty much fair and honest.

Algorithms don't lie to each other. But the further down the Forex food chain you go, the lower down the Maslow pyramid you also go.

Now, the fact that these banks abused their clients so blatantly, should give us all cause for concern. Financial institutions are our trusted fiduciaries. Unless you yourself are a bank, you place all your money and trust in this so called 'credible' institution called a bank. But just as this case will cause a number of reforms, so it may also shake up the thinking of clients, and their understanding of banking and fiduciary duty.

Respective authorities have announced remediation programs aimed at repairing trust in their banking systems and the wider foreign exchange market place. In the United Kingdom the FCA has stated that the changes to be made at each firm will depend on a number of factors, including the size of the firm, its market share, impact, remedial work already undertaken, and the role the firm plays in the market. The remediation program will require firms to review their IT systems in relation to their spot FX business, as the banks currently rely on legacy technologies that allow for the existence of dark-data silos within which manipulation is able to occur unnoticed by compliance systems.[31] In Switzerland the Swiss Financial Market Supervisory Authority has announced that for a period of two years UBS will be limited to a maximum annual variable compensation to 200% of the basic salary for foreign exchange and precious metals employees globally. UBS is instructed to automate at least 95% of its global foreign exchange trading, while effective measures must be taken to manage conflicts of interest with a particular focus on organizational separation of client and proprietary trading.

A bank license in many respects is sovereignty. If the banks have failed, if the banks have violated the public trust, maybe the public will reconsider their approach to banking. Banks were established by bankers, bankers used to be individuals, not institutions. Now, institutions hire bankers with outdated training to do jobs that mostly computer machines can now do. Maybe the public will do these Forex services for themselves, in the future.

The irony about the history of Forex and law in the United States, which may provide insights into why the Forex system in America is so controlled and dominated as if it is a Monopoly, is that the current Federal Reserve system was created in response to an inquiry into a small 'cabal' of bankers who controlled Wall St. During the Gilded Age, wealth was created that was never in the world seen before, in percent of GDP terms. The Congress of the United States created a subcommittee to investigate this control of the money system, called the Pujo Committee[xlviii]:

The Committee discovered several forces, such as the consolidation of banks and interlocking directorates (small groups of the same men serving as directors on several different boards) had led to increased wealth accumulation of 42.9% of America's total banking resources held by its twenty largest banks. Furthermore, with much surprise to the investigators, it was found that "180 individuals" covering "341 directorships in 112 corporations...[possessed] $22,245,000,000 in aggregate resources of capitalization." Finally, it was concluded that a system known counterintuitively as "Banking Ethics" prohibited competitions amongst banks and firms. Despite the fact that **lead attorney** Samuel Untermyer **had predetermined that no money trust would be found as part of the Investigation because "There is no agreement existing among these men that is in violation of the law"** and despite the refusal of aid by the Comptroller of the Currency, the failure of the Senate to pass the bill to amend section 5241 of the Revised Statutes and the lack of any authoritative decision by the courts sustaining the committee's right to access the books of the national banks, the Pujo Committee Report concluded in 1913 that a community of influential financial leaders had gained control of major manufacturing, transportation, mining, telecommunications and financial markets of the United States. The report revealed that at least eighteen different major financial corporations were under the control of a cartel led by J.P Morgan, George F Baker and James Stillman. These three men, through the resources of seven banks and trust companies (Banker's Trust Co., Guaranty Trust Co., Astor Trust Co., National Bank of Commerce, Liberty National Bank, Chase National Bank, Farmer's Loan and Trust Co.) controlled an estimated $2.1 billion. The report revealed that a handful of men held manipulative control of the New York Stock Exchange and attempted to evade interstate trade laws. The Pujo Report singled out individual bankers including Paul Warburg, Jacob H. Schiff, Felix M. Warburg, Frank E. Peabody, William Rockefeller and Benjamin Strong, Jr.. The report identified over $22 billion in resources and capitalization controlled through 341 directorships held in 112 corporations by members of the empire headed by J.P. Morgan. Although Pujo left Congress in 1913, the findings of the committee inspired public support for ratification of the Sixteenth Amendment in 1913, passage of the Federal Reserve Act that same year, and passage of the Clayton Antitrust Act in 1914.

In this context, the story about Jekyll Island isn't so far-fetched. But it outlines yet another Forex paradox, how the solution to a financial Monopoly was an even greater Monopoly. The "Money Trust" – a loosely organized group of bankers with similar interests consolidated their power into one central bank, the Federal Reserve. Fast forward 100 years, and Congress is investigating the Federal Reserve, and an "End the Fed" campaign attempts to reform the Federal Reserve System. In its most basic request, an attempt is being made to audit the Fed. Fed Chairman at the time, Ben Bernanke, said in front of Congress – "NO" when they asked for a list of banks who received Trillions of US Dollars from the Fed. Similar to the argument made during the Pujo committee, the Federal Reserve is under no legal obligation to open its books to Congress or any other third party. While it is true that the Fed was created by an act of Congress, their only official role with the Fed is that they are allowed to appoint the chairman. This chairmen though, once appointed, works independently, and is under no obligation to report to the President or any other government authority or entity. Mr. Bernanke was well within his duty to answer "NO" to Congress.

The difference between today's hearings and the Pujo Committee, is that now Congress gets billions of fresh

US Dollars from the Fed, so as long as this uber-conflict of interest exists, there will never be any serious Congressional investigation into our financial system.

And while there have been a series of anti-trust cases brought against the major Forex banks for anti-competitive practices, they often settle and continue doing more or less the same thing.

The settlement with Bank of America follows the plaintiffs' $135 million settlement with UBS, announced March 12, 2015, and the plaintiffs' $99.5 million settlement with JPMorgan, announced January 30, 2015. Bank of America, UBS, and JPMorgan have all agreed to cooperate with the plaintiffs in their continuing litigation against the nine remaining defendants. Hausfeld serves as co-lead plaintiffs' counsel with Scott + Scott LLP. Speaking on the settlement, Michael D. Hausfeld, Chairman at Hausfeld, stated, "Investors in the foreign exchange market that were harmed by Bank of America and the other defendants' anti-competitive actions can celebrate another win today. This settlement, which is the third announced since January, provides for substantial compensation as well as Bank of America's agreement to cooperate against the remaining banks.[xlix]"

Between all of these Forex cases, it's amazing that the large Forex banks continue to provide overall a terrible level of service at an extremely high cost. The fact is there isn't another choice – if you are based in the US and you have FX needs, you must choose one of the big Forex banks. Maybe judges don't understand Forex or maybe the cases just aren't enough to effect policy. In any case, it looks like there will be more problems before there will be a real Forex paradigm shift.

Forex Payments Case

Forex Payments, or deliverables, is when a domestic company needs to make a foreign payment in a foreign currency. Forex payments are referred to as 'deliverables' or 'payments' in the Forex trading community. In this case, the client usually instructs their bank to do this on their behalf. Most major banks, especially large money center banks, offer this service. Banks can charge up to 7% on Forex payment transactions. A number of banks (Bank of America, Bank One/First USA, Chase, Citibank, Diners Club, HSBC/Household, MBNA and Washington Mutual/Providian) recently settled a class action lawsuit [1] *"In re Currency Conversion Fee Antitrust Litigation"* but they continue to charge huge spreads on Forex payments.

How can the banks get away with it?

A few reasons; first, it's not illegal. Second, there are companies that offer reasonable rates on Forex payments (such as 1% instead of 7%) but very few use these services. Third, banks are overcharging on the spread, it's not actually a fee (although it becomes their profit). Since many don't understand how the Forex markets work, they don't calculate how much they are losing on these transactions. Finally, since banks are typically the source of funds, many people feel it's more convenient for the banks to process their Forex payments, or aren't aware there are alternatives.

What are spot rates?

When you trade Currency you must exchange one for another. Using an example of US Dollars to be exchanged for Euros, you would use the EUR/USD pair as a price reference. Forex traders who speculate in the market trade on spot rates, for example 1.3549 / 1.3551 – this is a 2 pip spread, or .02%. In the above mentioned case where banks charge 7%, this is roughly 700 pips making the spread 1.2849 / 1.4251. It's virtually impossible to get spot rates on a Forex payment transaction, however it is very possible to get close, which is referred to as 'near spot' which can depend on many factors including the currency in question, the size of the transaction, and the market price at that time.

So the real question is why do customers choose to lose 7% of their transaction value, when they can choose to lose only 1%? Because they don't understand Forex? Or because they are too lazy to use a Forex service? It is puzzling, how banks are able to charge such fees, settle lawsuits, and continue overcharging their customers.

4.3 Sophisticated Forex Investors (SFI)

Institutions, rich people, endowments, managed funds, family offices, and other groups that control a lot of money, are generally well trained in high finance. The average investor who really needs that money to pay their bills or for other purposes, really has no business investing. Investing should be done by those who can *really* afford to lose 100% of their investment, and for those who understand the risks involved. An entire industry 'financial services' now exists, with so many educational programs and certifications it is impossible to achieve them all in a lifetime. But Forex is completely left out! Only recently, the NFA offers Forex professionals the ability to get a Series 34 license, for Forex. While currencies are taught at high finance Universities, it is only taught in a broad sense, and based mostly on the pre-Nixon Forex market, using economic models that are even older.

To be blunt, there are very few Sophisticated Forex Investors in America. In the stock world, there are many sophisticated investors, too many to even describe. For various reasons, these Sophisticated Investors both never took the time to learn Forex and were never presented with a Sophisticated Forex investment. That's because there is a lack of professional grade, cutting edge Forex products in the United States of America. And to make things worse, there is a lack of Forex banks and brokers that even allow the retail investor to trade. The large Forex banks are involved in lawsuits and criminal investigations for Forex rigging, leaving virtually no one offering these savvy investors reliable Forex products & services, in America. In Europe, Asia, and other parts of the world, this is not the case! America has become a **big black Forex hole.** Although we cannot provide a certification, by reading this book in its entirety, you can consider yourself a **Sophisticated Forex Investors (SFI)**. While there will be no test per se, your portfolio is the real test! By your new found extensive Forex knowledge, you'll be able to hedge your Forex risks, hedge the risk of the collapsing US Dollar, and profit from Forex Managed Accounts. SFIs should be able to spot Forex risks on a 10-K filing and develop an appropriate strategy. Just imagine if you had invested in the Swiss Franc 15 years ago, more than doubling your money with no leverage, all the while gaining interest.

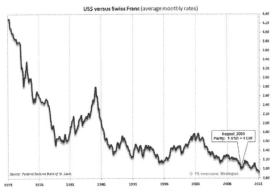

SFIs should most importantly, understand their functional accounting currency, and how to hedge the deterioration of its value. This chart of the USD/CHF is 2 sided – on the one hand, it shows how much money could have been made just by investing in the Swiss Franc. But on the other hand, it brightly shows how much real value the US Dollar has lost since the post-Nixon shock floating system. SFIs should understand that in Forex, if you're making money on such an investment in a foreign currency, you aren't gaining, you are just breaking even. In Forex, it's not about making money – that's for your core business. **Forex is about NOT LOSING,** including such subtle losses that are hard to account for, such as the deterioration of the US Dollar.

SFIs don't need a certification or a stamp, because the knowledge can be applied practically in life as an investor, businessman, and consumer. Forex is all about subtleties, such as the slow creeping effect of inflation. Inflation is called the hidden tax – but there's another subtlety that's a more damaging effect of inflation; deterioration of quality. Because companies cannot produce products year in and year out at the same price because of internal costs and out of control inflation, instead of raising the price to the consumer, they will decrease the quality. This can mean less chips in the Lays bag, or a pan that breaks on its first use. They are not so obvious, and usually very small changes. But over time, they can add up. And suddenly, 'premium' products are introduced, at 10x the price, with the same quality that was offered 20 years ago.

As is the case with many such situations, if all investors were SFIs, there would be less Forex fraud, less risk, and overall a more healthy financial system. Education, knowledge, and innovation are the only real drivers of markets; not regulation.

After finishing reading Splitting Pennies completely, you can consider yourself a Sophisticated Forex Investor (SFI). Owners of the book who have read it are entitled to a certificate.

To obtain your SFI certificate visit www.splittingpennies.com and register as an SP owner, and you will find instructions.

Congratulations!

5: Forex Magic – How to make money appear and disappear

What is the point of origin of any USD, whether paper or electronic? The answer is the Federal Reserve Bank. A central bank creates a currency. There are other currencies in use today such as local community currencies, corporate currencies like Disney Dollars (known as Corporate Scrip), and others. Bit Coin lends the most interesting example, as being completely electronic and backed by its encryption algorithm. Because the US Dollar is the global reserve currency, most other central banks use the USD model as a template. This describes modern times, it was not always the case. Various forms of money have been tested and used over the centuries.

Some interesting systems of note, the heaviest money used ever by the Yap islanders; Rai Stones[li]. Giant coins made of stone so large, they can only be transported by machine or in ancient times, by sizeable groups of men with tools. They are however rarely transported. Simply it's enough for them to agree that it's yours. They are mostly used only for significant social events such as inheritance, marriage, political deals, or signs of tribal alliance. It is an interesting example because they were so difficult to create and transport. It makes sense why such objects would be used as a currency. Also interesting, if someone died during the transport of one, it would become more valuable. This money was not fungible! Economist Milton Friedman has compared the monetary role of the stone money to the reserves of gold held in Fort Knox for foreign governments.

Fiat currencies such as the USD are simply in fashion. Even today, hundreds of local currencies, digital currencies, and barter are used on a daily basis. The IRS even provides rules to pay your taxes when you engage in Bit Coin transactions or barter. In fact, if you let your friend stay in your apartment for free, you are due to pay taxes on a barter transaction, based on the US Dollar rent value, or as determined by other services or goodwill value provided to you by said tenant.

Forex pertains currently to only Fiat currencies issued by countries, which form the basis of 99% of global trade. That means for the purposes of "Forex" discussion, we do not mention Bitcoin, Corporate Currencies, Community Currencies, or other modern currency inventions, however alluring and functional they are.

The Federal Reserve creates new money through lending. Thus, the US Dollar is a debt based currency. Mostly this is done on a wholesale level, to member banks. The member banks then lend this money at a premium to its customers.

Myth 43: America has an increasing debt and it should be paid off.

Reality: If we completely paid off all US Debt, including Government debt, corporate debt, and private debt – US money would cease to exist! In a debt based money system, it is necessary to issue more and more debt. The system is a finite system, but it is ever expanding. This is necessary to prevent implosion. Bankruptcy is built into the debt based money system. Like a game of musical chairs, inevitably, one player will be left without a chair when the music stops, such as Lehman Brothers in 2008.

The only way to analyze and modify such a system is through monetary policy only. Economic reforms, regulations, or other interventions are a complete waste of time. The only way to boost the economy is to give money to people. The power Elite recognized this after the legitimate attempt & failure of Dodd-Frank, Quantitative Easing, and other nonsense policies. They published their opinion in their favorite journal "Foreign Affairs" in an article titled "Print less but transfer more.[lii]"

It's well past time, then, for U.S. policymakers — as well as their counterparts in other developed countries — to consider a version of Friedman's helicopter drops. In the short term, such cash transfers could jump-start the economy. Over the long term, they could reduce dependence on the banking system for growth and reverse the trend of rising inequality. The transfers wouldn't cause damaging inflation, and few doubt that they would work. The only real question is why no government has tried them. The main reason governments have not tried this approach, say the authors, is the widespread belief that it will trigger hyperinflation. Unless one subscribes to the view that recessions are either therapeutic or deserved, there is no reason governments should not try to end them if they can, and cash transfers are a uniquely effective way of doing so. For one thing, they would quickly increase spending, and central banks could implement them instantaneously, unlike infrastructure spending or changes to the tax code, which typically require legislation. And in contrast to interest-rate cuts, cash transfers would affect demand directly, without the side effects of distorting financial markets and asset prices. They would also would help address inequality — without skinning the rich [liii]. Ideology aside, the main barriers to implementing this policy are surmountable. And the time is long past for this kind of innovation. Central banks are now trying to run twenty-first-century economies with a set of policy tools invented over a century ago. By relying too heavily on those tactics, they have ended up embracing policies with perverse consequences and poor payoffs. All it will take to change course is the courage, brains, and leadership to try something new.

This solution would solve economic problems overnight – but it requires a knowledge of Forex to see how easily it can work, and has nearly no down side. Practically what's been happening, the Fed creates new money and the banks keep it at the Fed for interest, getting some sort of unique arbitrage on several trillion held on deposit [liv].

There is a massive misconception about where the Bernanke Fed's stimulus landed. Although the Bernanke Fed has disbursed $2.284 trillion in new money (the monetary base) since August 1, 2008, one month before the 2008 financial crisis, **81.5 percent now sits idle as excess reserves in private banks**. The banks are not required to hold excess reserves. The excess reserves exploded from $831 billion in August 2008 to $1.863 trillion on June 14, 2013. The excess reserves of the nation's private banks had previously stayed at nearly zero since 1959 <u>as seen on the St. Louis Fed's chart</u>. The banks did not leave money idle in excess reserves at zero interest because they were investing in income earning assets, including loans to consumers and businesses. This 81.5 percent explosion in idle excess reserves means that the Bernanke Fed's new money issues of $85 billion each month have never been a big stimulus. Approximately 81.5 percent (or $69.27 billion) is either bought by banks or deposited into banks where it sits idle as excess reserves. The rest of the $85 billion, approximately 18.5 percent (or $15.72 billion) continues to circulate or is held as required reserves on banks' deposit accounts (unlike unrequired excess reserves).[iv]

The game of musical chairs

The fact that the money supply is ever increasing, means that money is constantly being devalued. That means investors NEED to beat inflation just to break even and maintain their savings. This puts investors into a situation where they constantly need to aggressively grow their portfolio. It's not because they are greedy, it's because their US Dollars are constantly being devalued! This drives investors to seek unreasonable rates of return, beyond what the economy can produce naturally. In other words, a debt based money system encourages unusually risky investing, pushes the limit of 'what's ethical' and makes average investors seek well above average rates of return.

One thing that people can do with their ever decreasing USD – they can buy Euros which hopefully is decreasing at a lesser rate. Of course, unless you live in Europe, you only care about the profits on the FX rate, but this is effectively what's happening with large capital flows in the Forex markets. Money is created by the central banks, some of which floods other currencies.

5.1 Fed Magic – Making Money

Imagine for a moment how the Federal Reserve creates new electronic money. Federal Reserve Notes (FRNs) are printed at the U.S. Mint which offers tours to the public. But the electronic systems used by the Fed need no tours – one can download their marketing materials from the Fed's website directly "Federal Reserve Bank Services [lvi] " frbservices.org Member banks and client banks who have an account with the Fed can request an unlimited amount of money at any time. With the current deposit ratio of zero for most instruments, and an interest rate of near zero, the Fed really is creating money out of nothing and giving it away for free. The post 2008 QE program created a strange arbitrage situation for the Fed's biggest client banks. The Fed loaned trillions of dollars to the banks at zero and near zero interest, but then allowed them to keep this money in a custody account at the Fed, which earned a small .5 or .75% interest rate, not more than one half of one percent or 50 basis points spread; but multiplied by trillions of dollars, this was a good source of profit for the banks – especially considering they did NOTHING for this money. The Fed claims that it didn't do this to shore up their balance sheets with easy profits, they claim that "QE Failed[lvii]" Here's what the creator of the QE program recently had to say on this topic:

Despite the Fed's rhetoric, my program wasn't helping to make credit any more accessible for the average American. The banks were only issuing fewer and fewer loans. More insidiously, whatever credit they were extending wasn't getting much cheaper. QE may have been driving down the wholesale cost for banks to make loans, but Wall Street was pocketing most of the extra cash.

From the trenches, several other Fed managers also began voicing the concern that QE wasn't working as planned. Our warnings fell on deaf ears. In the past, Fed leaders — even if they ultimately erred — would have worried obsessively about the costs versus the benefits of any major initiative. Now the only obsession seemed to be with the newest survey of financial market expectations or the latest in-person feedback from Wall Street's leading bankers and hedge fund managers. Sorry, U.S. taxpayer.

So – how does this magic work? The Federal Reserve has a software system that allows them to type numbers into a box, in any amount. This is how they create money. It's simple really – just enter 1,000,000,000,000 and now there is $1 Trillion USD more than there was 1 minute ago. From that point, they can send this money to any client bank they want, in any form they want, by clicking a button 'send.' Anyone who has online banking, who has done a transfer before or a bill payment, can imagine how this magic process works. There are many rules that are followed, bankers are generally groomed conservatively through all the right channels, to prevent the obvious conflict. But fraud exists, Fed workers are often caught with their hands in the cookie jar, or worse. In 2012, a "Mr. Zhang" was caught stealing code to a US Treasury software that handles accounting for entire sections of the US government, while he worked at the Reserve Bank of New York[lviii]:

*"Zhang took advantage of the access that came with his trusted position to steal highly sensitive proprietary software. **His intentions with regard to that software are immaterial.** Stealing it and copying it threatened the security of vitally important source code."* According to the complaint unsealed today in Manhattan federal court: The Government-Wide Accounting and Reporting Program ("GWA") is a software system that is owned by the United States Department of the Treasury ("DOT"). It is used principally to help keep track of the United States government's finances. Among other things, the GWA handles ledger accounting for each appropriation, fund, and receipt within the DOT, and provides federal agencies with an account statement—similar to bank statements provided to bank customers—of the agencies' account balances with the United States Treasury. The proprietary computer source code associated with the GWA is maintained by the Federal Reserve Board of New York ("FRBNY") in an access-controlled electronic repository. The FRBNY is further developing the source code for the GWA.

The FBI tells us that his intentions are immaterial, so we can expect that this was just a rogue employee, a unique situation that never happened before and would never happen again. It wasn't as if he was an agent for a foreign Asian government, or sponsored by an Elite rival banking clan in the east, or who knows what his intentions really were with this system?

In any event, this Windows based software is not much different than most users have on their home PCs. Fed employees, are not much different than average people. They make mistakes, they can be greedy – they are human beings! Because of the significance of the Federal Reserve, and the fact that Forex is not taught in school, there is much mystery and myth surrounding the Fed. The secrecy and mystery all started on a small island in the state of Georgia Christmas, 1910[lix]:

...in November of 1910 Senator Aldrich invited several bankers and economic scholars to attend a conference on Jekyll Island. While meeting under the ruse of a duck-shooting excursion, the financial experts were in reality hunting for a way to restructure America's banking system and eliminate the possibility of future economic panics. The 1910 "duck hunt" on Jekyll Island included Senator Nelson Aldrich, his personal secretary Arthur Shelton, former Harvard University professor of economics Dr. A. Piatt Andrew, J.P. Morgan & Co. partner Henry P. Davison, National City Bank president Frank A. Vanderlip and Kuhn, Loeb, and Co. partner Paul M. Warburg. From the start the group proceeded covertly. They began by shunning the use of their last names and met quietly at

Aldrich's private railway car in New Jersey. In 1916, B. C. Forbes discussed the Jekyll conference in his book Men Who Are Making America and illuminates, "To this day these financiers are Frank and Harry and Paul [and Piatt] to one another and the late Senator remained 'Nelson' to them until his death.

From another perspective[lx]:

Also in 1910, Senator Nelson Aldrich, Frank Vanderlip of National City (today know as Citibank), Henry Davison of Morgan Bank, and Paul Warburg of the Kuhn, Loeb Investment House met secretly at Jekyll Island, a resort island off the coast of Georgia, to discuss and formulate banking reform, including plans for a form of central banking. The meeting was held in secret because the participants knew that any plan they generated would be rejected automatically in the House of Representatives if it were associated with Wall Street. Because it was secret and because it involved Wall Street, the Jekyll Island affair has always been a favorite source of conspiracy theories. However, the movement toward significant banking and monetary reform was well-known.

Was all of this secrecy really necessary, or were bankers such as Paul Warburg simply obsessed with such behavior? Even today, the Elite engage in strange occult rituals, especially the higher up the pyramid you go. George Bush & John Kerry's "Skull & Bones" society is a great example. But does all this secrecy, elaborate hats and handshakes, really have any meaning, other than providing thrills to powerful men who are otherwise difficult to entertain? Where else can JP Morgan really have fun?

So we've learned that the Federal Reserve is not so mysterious at all, it's one of the most simple organizations on Wall St. Also it's one of the most efficient, in many ways. The Fed can create new USD as easy as you can type into Microsoft Excel the digits $1,000,000 and Whiz-Bang! New USD! Note that the Federal Reserve works ONLY with member banks & client banks. In order to receive this new currency, you must be a bank.

When it comes to Forex, this really becomes interesting. Domestic lending is a fairly known, limited market. The Fed does regional economic studies, which it knows basically where the money is. There can only be a reasonable amount of lending economically speaking, calculating for changing variables such as growing GDP, immigration, population growth, climate change, and so on.
Forex is another story.

5.2 Forex operations at the Fed
The Federal Reserve aggressively defends the value of the USD. Another Forex paradox – because the Fed on the one hand, constantly makes the value of the USD less and less by issuing more and more USD. Money supply is ever increasing. But on the other hand, the Fed doesn't want a situation where foreign market pressure could drive the value of the dollar down severely. The only thing central bankers don't like is volatility. The value of the USD is a two sided equation, domestically, and overseas. There are a huge amount of international corporations, governments, and other foreign entities that borrow in USD. Even with the use of hedging instruments,

ultimately, they must repay those loans in USD plus interest. So a weak dollar is in their favor, a strong dollar, is in the favor of the Fed. The Fed doesn't manipulate the value of the US Dollar directly via market operations (at least, we don't think so) such as other central banks do, but the Fed is very active in the Forex market via currency swap lines[lxi], overseas US Dollar funding & lending, and open market operations (OMO)[lxii].

The way currency swap lines work is simple. The Fed cannot create foreign currency, as it can create unlimited US Dollars. However, by agreement with other central banks, the Fed can provide to these central banks, unlimited quantities of US Dollars. This prevents havoc in the markets, if desperate investors were forced to buy US Dollars in the open market, it could drive down the value of the foreign currency severely, and drive up the value of the US Dollar, accordingly. In order to avoid this situation, the Federal Reserve will provide US Dollars to any foreign bank who asks. But this really shouldn't be called a 'swap' because in return for these trillions in US Dollars, the Fed asks nothing in return. Just please, use the US Dollars! The more global use of the US Dollar, the more reliance and legitimacy of the instrument is created.

Central Bank Liquidity Swaps - These swap facilities respond to the re-emergence of strains in short term funding markets. They are designed to improve liquidity conditions in global money markets and to minimize the risk that strains abroad could spread to U.S. markets, by providing foreign central banks with the capacity to deliver U.S. dollar funding to institutions in their jurisdictions and for the Federal Reserve to deliver foreign currency to U.S. institutions if conditions warrant. **At present, there is no need for the Federal Reserve to offer liquidity in foreign currencies.**

Since it is possible for the Fed to create unlimited money with its computer system, Fed market operations are irrelevant. The Fed takes no risk other than devaluing the currency. Inflation is a hidden tax. But like any vendor – the Fed works for its owners and customers successfully – banks. Banks want inflated asset prices, banks want the Fed to soak up toxic liquidity, and banks want the Fed to buy stocks if the market falls. The Fed has no interest in profits per se, because of this money creation machine. But its member banks do, and are always pressuring the Fed to do more, to enable them to make even more money. Electronic capitalism has gone parabolic.

Rumors persist, that the fed intervenes in markets in different ways. Sometimes it is rumored that the Fed props markets at key levels. This is apparently done by the Fed 'nudging' the market with large futures orders, from an anonymous account they control in the Caymans. By providing support of S&P futures for example, at key psychological levels, can really spoof the market into thinking that big investors are there buying and holding the market up like Atlas. If this is true, and there's no reason not to believe it, it is not difficult for the Fed to do this, considering its ability to create an unlimited supply of money. The plunge protection team (PPT) was announced publicly, but the nuances of how and when they do their job was never completely known. It isn't unreasonable to assume that a small group at the Fed has this job, and has setup systems in place that can prevent a stock market crash, for example. Anyway, the market is indirectly inflated by the QE money the Fed is printing and giving to banks & hedge funds, so what's the difference if the Fed steps in during a major sell off?

They do this publicly for their QE program, in that the fed openly buys MBS (Mortgage Backed Securities) and other instruments. Of course this policy is suspect, because the Fed should at some point unwind those positions, making the market worse than it was to begin with. Or the Fed can slowly own more and more of the financial assets of the United States ad infinitum.

While it's easy to manipulate the stock market, it's impossible to manipulate the Forex market! This is why the Fed has so much work if it wants to prop the dollar. The Fed can't simply go into the market and buy dollars (like it can stocks or other instruments). So the Fed must work closely with other central banks – most importantly – the ECB (European Central Bank) who now has a Fed Chairman who conveniently has a PhD from an American university, MIT. Also, Dr. Draghi has an extensive connection to the US, being involved with universities such as Harvard, and working for Goldman Sachs. The Euro – very similar to the US Dollar! At least for the near future, it seems these 2 super currencies are a match made in heaven, with no competition or threats of their global financial supremacy.

5.3 Why and how the average person loses money in Forex

Retail Forex is not Forex at all – it's an illusion. The only way to really trade Forex is with a bank. Brokers provide a hobby environment for the average investor to play around and learn something and eventually lose money. Very few retail accounts have made a significant profit and those that have, resulted in issues with the broker processing withdrawal requests.

How to lose money in the forex market

1. The average investor feels the pressure of the debasing of the currency. They feel it in their portfolios, and at the grocery store, and when they send their kids to school. The average investor is pressured to find unusually risky strategies not offered by the traditional establishments. Mutual Funds are not going to beat real inflation. Charles Schwab doesn't offer Binary Options. So the average investor searches the internet looking for 10% per month returns. During the period of 2004 – 2010, hundreds of scam Forex companies touted huge returns, which were a combination of outright frauds, or bad traders who just exaggerated their numbers. There was no regulation, it was the Wild West. 95% of these self-proclaimed managers were complete frauds. Investors lost millions.

2. There is a huge learning curve with Forex trading. Of course it's possible to make a fortune trading Forex – banks do it every day. But for the average investor, who doesn't have a background in mathematics, quantum physics, econometrics, or game theory; it's not so easy. They are misled to believe by 'professionals' selling courses for $5,000 and more that they too can make millions in the Forex market. These marketers of course, make money by selling courses, not by trading. So

there exists an information paradox – these retail investors search the internet for Forex knowledge, but find only marketers who are selling their product. These marketers are very good marketers! But unfortunately for the client, they are only good at marketing, and nothing more. There are few places if any, which offer unbiased Forex information.

3. Retail Forex brokers play dirty games with clients. Knowing that most clients will lose, they will encourage clients to lose even more than they normally would. How can they do this? In Forex, contrasted with other markets, clients trade against the broker. That means the broker or bank is the counterparty to the client. It's in the legal agreements, and it's in the software. What normal honest Forex ECNs do, they pass orders on to another matching order or exchange; this is known as STP (Straight Through Processing). But brokers would only make a small commission on an STP order, whereas if they take the other side of the client order and win, their profit is the clients' loss. Many retail Forex traders simply do not trade properly and are subject to gamblers ruin or common human emotion trading issues. Knowing this, brokers act as market dealing desks which take risk on client orders, betting that the clients will be wrong. Just as the client has a trading terminal, the dealer has a trading terminal – but the dealer can see all the clients' orders, stop losses, and other information. If the dealer feels obliged, he can always offset client risk in the open interbank market. If the dealer is wrong, it can be catastrophic for the broker. In rare cases, when brokers have been desperate,

they have simply reversed positive client orders at the roll (5pm NY/EST). When clients call to complain or become angry, they close the client account and refer the client to their high priced lawyers (in many cases, these are some of the highest crust lawyers in global finance that money can buy). Many of them claim they are not doing this 'trading against clients' when they have really just found another way to do it. Strategies include price shifting, price leaning, platform freezing, error message flashing, negative slippage, off-quotes, and the most severe – account statement 'reconciliation.' At the end of the day, for the client – the Forex market is what the broker says it is. During the 'golden years' of retail US Forex, it was possible to notice price discrepancies between 5 different brokers. Literally, it was possible to run the identical strategy in algorithmic form at 10 brokers and get 10 completely different results! One common algorithm used by dealers to mitigate their human risk was called "Virtual Dealer" which was a broker plugin offered by the MetaQuotes company from Kazan, Russia. These practices evolve over time, but always remain of the same nature. The point is that clients didn't have a fair chance to trade Forex purely. Although brokers have improved their level of service, clients still lose more than win. Statistics of client losses in the past 10 years as provided by brokers have moved from 95% to 60% - meaning that 10 years ago, 95% of retail Forex clients were losing.

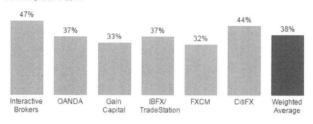

Profitable Accounts

In the U.S., more than six in 10 customers at the retail foreign-exchange brokerages lost money in the third quarter of 2014.

According to the Wall St. Journal, 6 in 10 retail Forex traders are losing[lxiii]. Even though it is an improvement from 9 out of 10, it is still a staggering number. Some of these 'losses' are significant. But what is causing these losses? Is it just because Forex is so complicated, and so misunderstood? Partly, but also it is because these brokers play games with clients in order to make more money for themselves. Just as clients have a front end strategy to make money in Forex, whatever it may be, the brokers have a back end strategy to make money from clients. The fact that "Forex" is in between the client and the broker is completely irrelevant. It's technically speaking, no different than book keeping, spread betting. This is an unfortunate state of affairs, particularly for the client.

The games that these retail brokers play are extremely technical. As Forex is completely an electronic market, with no exchange, the Forex market as experienced by customers is defined by the broker, and the Software Company or internal team used to develop this platform. Even with the proliferation of the popular Meta Trader 4 MT4 platform, each broker offers a different environment – different spreads, different pairs, different tools to trade. Some brokers choose to close during times of economic news releases, for 10 minutes before and after a news release. Others may simply widen the spreads. Their games are always changing and evolving, just like the Forex market itself.

The demographic profile of these clients varies greatly. Some are just curious about Forex, others may be looking for alternative ways to invest. The most toxic Forex profile though are referred to as "Back Alley Dicers." They are not only clients, they are also Ponzi scammers and Forex professionals. Clinically, these individuals probably just have a gambling problem. Unfortunately, Forex provides the perfect online casino for them. It's open 24/6 and there are usually more than 20 or 30 pairs offered by the broker/bank, with huge leverage. What makes Forex even more addicting for these types is Binary Options – when traders can bet if the price of EUR/USD will be 'up or down' in 60 seconds. For some reason Forex attracts people like this, and they've given Forex a bad name in the US especially. But do not think back alley dicers are limited only to retail – bank traders such as the London Whale doubled down on bets the size of small countries[lxiv].

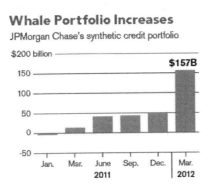

Whale Portfolio Increases
JPMorgan Chase's synthetic credit portfolio

This type of trading is the topic for a series of psychological journal articles, not a financial book.

The behaviors of gamblers are common across the wide range of Forex traders, institutional and retail. Fortunately, this has never happened on a very large scale (for example, at a central bank) of any significance. The central bank that holds the Guinness Book record for the highest inflation is Zimbabwe[lxv], with inflation rates above millions of percent. It is the best example of a fiat currency gone out of control, with the Central Bank printing currency so quickly that they regularly 'reset' the zeros on bills. In 2008 the inflation rate of the Zimbabwe dollar was 231,150,888.87% in one year!

Date	Rate
2004	132.75%
2005	585.84%
2006	1,281.11%
2007	66,212.3%
2008 Jul.	231,150,888.87%

It is laughable, because it is a number so large and ridiculous, it seems not real. But it is the financial reality for those who live and do business in Zimbabwe. Ironically, this extreme hyperinflation was caused by financial reforms suggested by the World Bank and the IMF, which led to their acceptance of the use of the US Dollar as their currency. Slowly, the US Dollar itself is become a one world currency!

Part of the Forex paradox, there is always a push and pull effect for any currency pair. With only a few rare exceptions such as Zimbabwe, currencies usually have opposing forces driving them back to where they started, like gravity and anti-gravity. Politically, policy always favors exporters – but importers too want a strong currency to be able to buy foreign products cheap. Exporter countries such as Japan, have an obvious need for a weak currency, which has been reflected in their Forex policy by the BOJ (Bank of Japan) over the last several decades. Being the world's reserve currency, the US Dollar always is more complicated than other currencies, but generally the US has always favored a 'strong dollar policy.' When central banks of the world decide to make their Forex magic and create or destroy money, they consider Forex ramifications probably more than anything else. Because **Forex determines the real value of their money, on the world marketplace.**

6: Forex Economics

Forex impacts economics today almost more than any other element. Certainly Forex is the most important market that impacts economics & other markets, stock valuations, and all other aspects of the modern economy. This was not always the case. The recent opening of BRIC (Brazil, Russia, India, & China) countries for trade, in parallel with explosive internet penetration in emerging markets, have made the world almost completely flat.   Thomas Friedman explains this transformation of the global economy in his book "The world is flat"[lxvi] (Friedman, 2005):

Ten flatteners
Friedman defines ten "flatteners" that he sees as leveling the global playing field:

- *#1: <u>Collapse of the Berlin Wall</u> – 11/9/89: Friedman called the flattener, "When the walls came down, and the windows came up." The event not only symbolized the end of the <u>Cold War</u>, it allowed people from the other side of the wall to join the economic mainstream. "11/9/89" is a discussion about the Berlin Wall coming down, the "fall" of communism, and the impact that Windows powered PCs (personal computers) had on the ability of individuals to create their own content and connect to one another. At that point, the basic platform for the revolution to follow was created: IBM PC, Windows, a standardized graphical interface for word processing, dial-up modems, a standardized tool for communication, and a global phone network.*

- **#2:** _Netscape_ – **8/9/95**: Netscape went public at the price of $28. Netscape and the Web broadened the audience for the Internet from its roots as a communications medium used primarily by "early adopters and geeks" to something that made the Internet accessible to everyone from five-year-olds to ninety-five-year-olds. The digitization that took place meant that everyday occurrences such as words, files, films, music, and pictures could be accessed and manipulated on a computer screen by all people across the world.
- **#3:** _Workflow software_: Friedman's catch-all for the standards and technologies that allowed work to flow. The ability of machines to talk to other machines with no humans involved, as stated by Friedman. Friedman believes these first three forces have become a "crude foundation of a whole new global platform for collaboration." There was an emergence of software protocols (SMTP – simple mail transfer protocol; HTML – the language that enabled anyone to design and publish documents that could be transmitted to and read on any computer anywhere) Standards on Standards. This is what Friedman called the "Genesis moment of the flat world." The net result "is that people can work with other people on more stuff than ever before." This created a global platform for multiple forms of collaboration. The next six flatteners sprung from this platform.
- **#4:** _Uploading_: Communities uploading and collaborating on online projects. Examples include open source software, blogs,

and Wikipedia. Friedman considers the phenomenon "the most disruptive force of all."

- **#5: Outsourcing**: Friedman argues that outsourcing has allowed companies to split service and manufacturing activities into components which can be subcontracted and performed in the most efficient, cost-effective way. This process became easier with the mass distribution of fiber optic cables during the introduction of the World Wide Web.

- **#6: Offshoring**: The internal relocation of a company's manufacturing or other processes to a foreign land to take advantage of less costly operations there. China's entrance in the WTO (World Trade Organization) allowed for greater competition in the playing field. Now countries such as Malaysia, Mexico, and Brazil must compete against China and each other to have businesses offshore to them.

- **#7: Supply-chaining**: Friedman compares the modern retail supply chain to a river, and points to Wal-Mart as the best example of a company using technology to streamline item sales, distribution, and shipping.

- **#8: Insourcing**: Friedman uses UPS as a prime example for insourcing, in which the company's employees perform services – beyond shipping – for another company. For example, UPS repairs Toshiba computers on behalf of Toshiba. The work is done at the UPS hub, by UPS employees.

- **#9: Informing**: Google and other search engines and Wikipedia are the prime example. "Never before in the history of the planet have so many people – on their own – had the ability to find so much information about so many things and *about so many other people," writes Friedman. The growth of search engines is tremendous; for example, Friedman states that Google is "now processing roughly one billion searches per day, up from 150 million just three years ago."*

- *#10: "The Steroids": Wireless, Voice over Internet, and file sharing. Personal digital devices like mobile phones, iPods, personal digital assistants, instant messaging, and voice over Internet Protocol (VoIP). Digital, Mobile, Personal and Virtual – all analog content and processes (from entertainment to photography to word processing) can be digitized and therefore shaped, manipulated and transmitted; virtual – these processes can be done at high speed with total ease; mobile – can be done anywhere, anytime by anyone; and personal – can be done by you.*

In a global connected flat economy, Forex is the grease that allows this machine to operate. Many consumers do not see this. As retailers want to make the process seamless for consumers, the Forex elements are handled on a wholesale basis. So when consumers go into Wal-Mart to buy a pair of their favorite socks made in China, they don't pay in Yuan they pay in US Dollars.

There are more stark examples in the industrial economy. A group of ancient samurais who live in a monastery on a mountaintop in rural Japan (metaphorically speaking, but almost) is the only source of critical nuclear fuel rods in the entire world[lxvii].

<u>Japan Steel Works</u> is the worlds only volume builder of nuclear reactor vessels, the steel container that holds radioactive fuel, and in case of a meltdown, prevents that fuel from leaking and triggering a catastrophe. Founded in 1907 and rebuilt following World War II, it supplied nearly all of the vessels used in Japan's 54 nuclear power plants, including the containers at the Fukushima Daiichi plants designed by General Electric and Toshiba. While those vessels were made from steel plates bolted and welded together, modern designs require Japan Steel Works to forge containers from a single ingot that can weigh up to 600 tons. It's a slow process that takes months at a time, using the company's 14,000-ton press to shape a special steel alloy that's been purified to maximize its strength. These methods also minimize seams that can give way in case of a meltdown, where nuclear fuel can reach 2,000 degrees Celsius. **Although Japan Steel Works is a major corporation with 5,000 employees, it also maintains a samurai sword blacksmith, in a small shack on a hill above the factory in Muroran, where a single craftsman still hammers steel into broadswords, as the company has done since 1917.** The expertly crafted swords, which sell for about 1 million yen when finished, are forged from a single 2.2-lb. lump of Tamahagane steel, the traditional material that's rarely used today. "Samurai swords contain the essence of steelmaking technology," Japan Steel Works CEO Masahisa Nagata <u>told Bloomberg</u> in 2008.

Those nuclear rods built by Japan Steel Works are used in every Nuclear power plant in the world. Built and manufactured in Yen, sold in US Dollars, Euros, Russian Ruble, Great British Pounds, and Chinese Yuan. This is the global economy that makes Forex the focus point.

Forex enables for this process a financing mechanism, payment system, and even hedging options. By purchasing Forex Forwards, the manufacturer can secure a static price for months or even years into the future (probably, the pricing of Forwards for more than 12 months may not exist or be cost efficient, but options could always be used accomplishing the same thing).

This mechanism enables countries that manufacture absolutely nothing (like Malta) to have absolutely everything. There's no reason that a global citizen cannot purchase any item on the planet and have it shipped anywhere. Those with experience in extreme emerging markets know that FedEx, for a fee, can even pickup an object (such as a laptop) at remote office locations. Phones such as Iridium Satellite Phones [lxviii] work in Pakistan, the Arctic, or in the Himalayas. Doing business & travelling on planet Earth has become convenient, even in remote locations. Forex makes this all possible.

Economic myth 98: The US has a trade deficit only because Americans are big spenders and debt hoarders.

It is difficult to measure the international economic impact of a country that serves as the world reserve currency, due to the Triffin Dilemma [lxix]. Because the US Dollar is used as a world reserve currency, and because of the Petro Dollar system where Oil is priced and sold in US Dollars, there is a constant foreign need for US Dollars. That means as a matter of economic necessity, the Fed is forced to create currency and provide it where it is needed. This increases the money supply, and thus the trade deficit. While this paradox was noted in 1960 before the floating exchange system we have today, the global use of the US Dollar as a reserve, should be noted, as its impact on the global economy is profound. Most recently, the Fed created tens of trillions of US Dollars for the Quantitative Easing (QE) program, nearly half of which went to European banks. Probably, they really needed US Dollars. In any event, these dollars were used outside the US economic system.

6.1 How Forex impacts the economy
The economy is often measured with domestic – single currency economic numbers. Even studies such as econometrics use scientific methods, and formulas which are very good – but do not consider the Forex element. In fact, few economic analysis considers the value of money at all.

Take a look at any standard economic indicator, and you will see Forex implications behind. The most obvious indicator, pertaining to the value of money itself, and that affects every economic actor, is that of inflation. Forex impacts inflation directly because as a currency is perceived to be less valuable, it will be exchanged for another currency, driving the value down more. This can be seen most acutely in emerging markets (EM) – in many EM, economic actors will use a stable, foreign currency such as the Euro or US Dollar (depending on their cultural background). The most ironic and paradoxical example of this is Cuba. While the United States maintained an economic embargo on the small island, which is now in talks of being lifted; the Cuban people used the US Dollar as their primary currency.

Castro, while being enemy #1 of the United States, was in the same moment, the best customer of the United States.

Although Castro has replaced the U.S. dollar with the **Cuban convertible peso, or CUC**, Cuba has always operated under a de facto dollarized economy. The CUC is an internationally unsupported currency, and it is, for all intents and purposes, pegged to the U.S. dollar. All of the CADECA branches and major banks will change U.S. dollars, euros, British pounds, and Canadian dollars. There are, in fact, two distinct kinds of currency circulating in Cuba: the moneda libremente convertible ("convertible peso" or CUC), and the moneda nacional (Cuban peso or MN or CUP). Both are distinguished by the dollar $ symbol, leading to some confusion. Both the CUC and moneda nacional are divided up into units of 100 centavos. To complicate matters, the euro is also legal tender in many of the hotels, restaurants, and shops in several of the larger, isolated beach resort destinations. **Note:** In this guide, we list prices in the Cuban convertible peso (CUC$), but when an establishment only accepts the Cuban peso (MN) we also list prices in MN[lxx].

Foreign loans can be impacted greatly by Forex. Due to its huge banking sector, the United States itself has almost no foreign loans. It's impossible for a US Citizen to establish a foreign loan. This can also be a contributing factor to the Forex intellectual void in the US. But foreign loans outside of the US are quite common. Also, US banks engage in huge amounts of foreign loans, often denominated in US Dollars. The largest market is that of US Treasuries. There's often talk in the news about foreign governments holding this debt.

MYTH 1982: Foreign countries hold some sort of power over the United States because of all this debt they hold.

REALITY: If the Fed wanted to, they could pay off the debt in 1 minute, by printing electronically the exact amount of the US debt, call in the bonds and payoff investors. It has been done before (although on a smaller scale).

Let's be 'Forex' about this topic – there is no threat from China or any other country that they hold US Debt. The US has the power to default on it; or – the Fed can simply print all the money necessary to repay all this debt in one swift keystroke, and no more debt. Foreign governments hold no authority and gain no power whatsoever by holding US Treasuries.   They have only risk. This would not be the case if the US Dollar was not the reserve currency, and the leading military power in the world. For example, imagine a scenario where the US defaults and the US Dollar plummets. It would change little in the domestic market, after a few years of reorganizing the local economy, the US could be import dependent, energy independent, and once again, an isolationist. This is not a likely scenario, but this simple thought experiment provides a more objective view of the situation that foreigners have some subtle agenda by acquiring this debt, as if it could be used for political purposes. For example, in a default scenario, foreign powers are not going to come to the US and seize critical assets in some sort of international fire sale.

There's just no scenario where these bond holders can exert any sort of power over the US Government by holding these bonds. The fact is, the US Government is considered creditworthy, mostly because it is the largest military power in the world, and it never defaulted – but most importantly because it maintains the global reserve currency – the US Dollar. And as far as the bond market goes – Treasuries are not such a bad investment, at least if you want to get your money back. In a ZIRP (Zero Interest Rate Policy) environment, even the German government sold billions in bonds with a NEGATIVE rate[lxxi]! Investors are paying, that they can be assured to get their money back, well at least 99% of it.

But while the Treasury market is interesting, it isn't the only part of the global US debt market. US and Foreign banks alike issue much US debt, in many forms. This includes commercial paper, traditional mortgage loans, business financing, government loans, and key development loans; such as offered by the World Bank. As the loans are denominated in US Dollars, as the dollar becomes stronger, it puts pressure to repay these loans. Probably, some of these loans include Forex hedging elements, but as we can see from corporate earnings releases of publicly traded companies, most do not.

Outside the US, the international loan market – or we can call it **the Forex Debt Market** – is very active. It exists from any country to any country, literally – with only extreme exceptions like North Korea who live in their own world. It is especially popular with ex colonial powers such as Holland, France, Great Britain, Spain, and Portugal. As first publicly acknowledged in an academic journal "**If Not by Tanks, Then by Banks?** The

Role of Soft Power in Putin's Foreign Policy" by Andrei P. Tsygankov, Europe-Asia Studies, Vol. 58, No. 7 (Nov., 2006), pp. 1079-1099. While the article is an analysis specifically of Putin's power projection on ex-Soviet states, it captures the thinking of the European Elite perhaps for the last 60 years. Germany is a great example of this, because they are not allowed to have tanks. And they are very active bankers in other countries. German banks provide a huge amount of foreign loans to surrounding countries. Especially popular in countries with less developed banking systems and exotic currencies, Northern European banks dominate the lending scene. But since these banks are not from these countries, the majority of their loans are Forex loans. A strong move in the currency, can bankrupt entire businesses, and have many disastrous consequences for the economy.

6.2 Government lies

Government economic indicators are manipulated for political purposes. Politicians use this as a tool to get votes and keep the population docile. Governments release economic indicators that impact Forex markets, but many of those numbers are influenced by Forex. It's a two way relationship. In Forex, the most significant economic data release in any currency, is the feared NFP (Non-Farm Payrolls). Practically, NFP doesn't directly impact Forex such as an interest rate announcement, or Fed 'jawboning' about a policy change. But the perception in the market is that if NFP beats the estimates, dollar up; if it fails, dollar down. The unique thing about NFP - the market can gap 100 or 200 pips in the blink of an eye. Some brokers even widen the spread during this time, and traders will shut down their algos only to restart them after markets calm down. Ironically, **the NFP number is completely manipulated!** Government lies and manipulation of economic data have become another tool to gain political power without directly taxing the people. Like inflation, the hidden tax, the manipulation of economic data is so subtle, it would be difficult to amount any prosecution against them, or even a debate. Because, according to the thinking – NFP is correct. And it is. But it's what is NOT in the data, and how it's calculated, where the deception lies. Non-Farm Payrolls should calculate job growth in the United States, minus cotton picking workers[lxxii]:

Nonfarm payroll employment is a compiled name for goods, construction and manufacturing companies in the US. It does not include farm workers, private household employees, or non-profit organization employees.

America has a history of using jobs as a means of growth, and as a focus of economic analysis. Because there is little disagreement that jobs are good for families and for the economy. Workers earn money and spend money.

NFP numbers are manipulated in many ways – but most importantly, it has a strict, difficult to qualify for criteria. Most obviously, if someone who is fired and seeks employment and never finds a job, after a certain period, they are no longer counted towards the unemployed. Unemployed persons, according to this methodology, are those who only recently graduated university or who have recently been laid off. But this is no longer a secret. Even some have made a business out of this discrepancy, such as John Williams, publisher of www.shadowstats.com

"John Williams' Shadow Government Statistics" is an electronic newsletter service that exposes and analyzes flaws in current U.S. government economic data and reporting, as well as in certain private-sector numbers, and provides an assessment of underlying economic and financial conditions, net of financial-market and political hype.[lxxiii]

For a fee, clients can access realistic economic data, as interpolated by their research team. Unemployment is the largest discrepancy but not the only one. How agencies, governments, and institutions calculate and release such data has become a source of manipulation. Maybe it was a bad idea to show "Trading Places" in economics classes – while the story provides a good lesson about the realities of the markets, it may have given rise to a generation of "Mr. Beeks."

In figure 4, a man is depicted using an anonymous payphone to contact his client, who wants to know the content of the crop report, before it is released (which is the equivalent of seeing the future, in trading).

Unemployment has hovered below 10% for some time, as of this writing, is 5.7% as calculated and published by the Bureau of Labor Statistics.[lxxiv] But considering what we can call 'real unemployment' which has been cleverly branded 'non-working' rather than 'unemployed' – based on the 'labor force participation rate' – the number is more like 40% or more. 94 Million Americans who are eligible to work are not in the 'labor force' – but they aren't counted as 'unemployed.[lxxv]' Maybe they choose not to work, or they are just lazy, or according to the Atlanta Fed, **They just don't want a job[lxxvi]:**

*The decrease in labor force participation among prime-age individuals **has been driven mostly by the share who say they currently don't want a job.** As of December 2014, prime-age labor force participation was 2.4 percentage points below its prerecession average. Of that, 0.5 percentage point is accounted for by a higher share who indicate they currently want a job; 2 percentage points can be attributed to a higher share who say they currently don't want a job.*

Of course, the simple solution – economically speaking, now agreed by world intellectuals and even Elite groups like the CFR (Council on Foreign Relations), is to simply give these out of work individuals money, which they would immediately spend[lxxvii].

Governments have a unique relationship with markets, and at the heart of markets is economic data. Currently governments have huge incentives with little political risk by manipulating economic data, for a plethora of motivations. At all market points, it seems there is government intervention in Forex. They regulate the banks and brokers, they release key economic data, and they give authority to central banks.

6.3 The corporate slumber

Publicly traded companies around the world have a horrible track record when it comes to Forex. With few exceptions, corporations rise and fall with the tide of their domestic currency. A strong dollar is bad for exporters, a weak dollar is bad for importers. "Currency Headwinds" is a recent buzzword that CFO's (Chief Financial Advisors) use to legitimize their Forex losses. Why these huge corporation cannot hedge themselves is a mystery that can only be explained by psychologists. But simply – the excuse works! Any of these Public companies could hire an FX manager to hedge their Forex positions, and in many cases even profit. But if the leaders of these Public companies don't understand Forex, it is a quandary for them. They'd rather not deal with something they don't understand, as long as they don't have to. They have no political incentives to explore Forex. They have a HUGE financial incentive – they not only have a fiduciary duty to shareholders, but CEO's (Chief Executive Officers) are usually paid tied to performance. This means that when Public companies have losses due to Forex, CEO's make less money. But they risk no persecution for not exploring Forex, so they'd rather let sleeping dogs lie.

Let's take a look at a recent Herbalife Ltd. (HLF) financial filing, from TheStreet.com[lxxviii]:

Herbalife Ltd. Announces Fourth Quarter and Full Year 2015 Results

- Fourth quarter adjusted1 EPS of $1.19 per diluted share and reported EPS of $0.98 per diluted share
- Fourth quarter volume points grew 5% compared to prior year
- **Fourth quarter reported net sales of $1.1 billion, increased 9.7% in local currency and declined 3.1% on a reported basis compared to the prior year period due to the unfavorable impact of currency exchange rates**
- Cash flow from operations during the quarter was $135.5 million and for the full year was $628.7 million
- Annual sales leader retention of approximately 54.2% percent
- **Due to the continued adverse impact from currency exchange rates, full year 2016 adjusted diluted EPS guidance is now expected to be in a range of $4.05 to $4.50, which reflects a $0.80 currency headwind compared to the prior year**

There isn't much to elaborate here – HLF should hire a Forex expert and create a hedging system, to eliminate "Currency Headwinds." It's really simple to do this, for those who understand Forex. It is simply amazing that a publicly traded company can be so reckless with billions of dollars. What is also strange is that aside from the fiduciary duty to shareholders, C level executives face strong pressure from investors to perform, especially from activist hedge fund investors. So one would think, that eliminating a billion dollar loss or multi-billion dollar loss by simply using basic Forex hedging, would behoove them.

Does this corporate slumber illustrate the lack of Forex understanding by corporate America? Or do CEOs use Forex as an accounting excuse for bad performance generally?

These executives are paid millions of dollars to provide the best management services possible, as much as $84 Million in one year.[lxxix] One would think that with this level of service, they would be competent enough to employ a currency hedging system. Currency hedging can be active or passive, but in any case, it can be setup in such a way that eliminates this balance sheet risk. It would cost the company – like an insurance premium. But public companies carry many types of corporate insurance – even for strange legal situations with a very low chance of occurrence. Why not Forex? A company has sold 30,000 policies for Alien Abduction[lxxx]; insurance companies will insure anything. Even without considering Forex hedging, it's certain that Forex insurance products could be organized by such companies.

Dodd-Frank regulations stipulated that public companies must administer "Internal Controls over Financial Reporting" to manage risk[lxxxi]. At some point, an argument could be made that lack of Forex hedging could be a violation of this rule. It is simply reckless to lose billions of dollars because of a lack of Forex hedging.

6.4 USD as debt based money

Nothing can impact the real economy more than the financial system. In reality, banks need the economy – the economy doesn't need banks. But the banks have sold us that we need their financial products that they invented – that do not exist. Business needs a means of counting their beans – in US Dollars.

The high level perspective is always monetary policy. Many economists believe that through the analysis of monetary policy all can be understood. The US Dollar is a debt based money system because all new currency is issued via loans. The Fed doesn't print money and throw it out of helicopters, as some have proposed. Because of this debt based system, it is constantly necessary to repay the Fed more dollars than initially were issued. This means that bankruptcy is built into the economic model. This characterizes businesses, their behavior, and their doctrine. Because if they don't earn above average returns, they can't grow and they can't pay off their debt.

This may sound strange, but it's only because we are not taught how the US Dollar functions in such detail. There are other examples of money that are not debt based, for example a gold backed currency – or Gold itself as a currency.

Any business who uses the US Dollar is subject to pressure to perform because of the deteriorating value, and because of the interest repayment paradox. The debt in total outstanding in US Dollars can never be paid off completely, because it would destroy money. Literally, the financial system in US Dollars would implode. Other currencies would flourish, but that's another story. A debt based money system pressures businesses to at least beat the competition, as in a game of musical chairs.

Ergo, the fundamental economic problem facing the world is Forex management, not offshoring or globalization.

7: Making Money in Forex

Central banks print as much money as they want. But if you know Forex – so can you! But first a small note about this famous idiomatic expression 'make money'. Making money read explicitly, is illegal. It's called counterfeiting and involves prison time. What can we do to profit from Forex, and protect ourselves?

Forex is the single biggest business market in the world, and it's right in your pocket. The USD is a monopoly – and Americans aren't seizing the opportunity.

A simple breakdown of the ways to make money in Forex, legally:

- Invest in Forex, such as a managed account
- Exploit a Forex strategy
- Make a business out of Forex

In the United States, almost all aspects of Forex is regulated on a retail level, which means for the average person to participate, they must choose a US based regulated broker. If they themselves want to be a Forex professional, they should have the Series 3 and Series 34 license, to work with clients (if you work for a big bank, they won't require that you are licensed as you'll mostly be front running client orders).

But there are a number of ways that anyone can participate in the Forex market, ranging from signal services to managed accounts. Trading Forex for yourself is not advisable, for reasons that should be

SPLITTING PENNIES – *Understanding Forex*

understood by this point in the book. But if you are going to have a go at it – do it properly. Take the time required to learn, develop a strategy, and make a business out of it. Unlike other markets, in Forex it's all a net positive for the industry! Unlike other markets, in Forex there is no competition, because Forex is not a zero sum market. If there are 10,000 US managers in Forex they would have 10,000 different strategies. It is possible that they could all win, irrespective of market movement. This simply isn't possible in other markets, which is what makes Forex so unique.

7.1 Developing a winning Forex Strategy

Broadly speaking, it's possible for any retail investor, corporate executive, or banker to develop a winning Forex strategy for themselves or for their institution.

First, define your goals – what do you want to achieve? Second, begin a self-imposed education regime. It's important to learn all aspects of this process, down to the computers you'll be using (or not using, depending on what you want to achieve). Building a Forex knowledgebase as a precursor is necessary for any strategy. It seems that in Forex, even those who win – only do so for a certain time period, and one little detail they forgot causes everything to unravel. At least basic knowledge of computing, options, and money are required.

Suggested Syllabus for becoming a Forex master:

1. Banking & Finance
2. History of Forex
3. IT & Computers
4. Compliance, Regulation & Ethics

5. Economics & Analysis
6. FX Business
7. Algorithmic Trading Systems

3 Basic types of Forex involvement:

- **Forex Speculation** – Profit by changes in the currency market
- **Forex Hedging** – Protect your assets, or your portfolio, by using tools such as options, forwards, and futures
- **Forex Business** – Open a Forex business or get a Forex job

Forex Hedging is highly specific to the needs of your current financial operations. Companies that do business internationally in multiple currencies, need to have an active hedging regime. There are 2 basic types of hedging, active and passive. Passive hedging means just buying options or forwards as you need FX. Active hedging means that the manager takes an active role in the contracts, and develops a strategy as would a trader. By using active hedging techniques, it is possible to achieve profits without taking additional risk, if the market moves in a certain direction – usually driven by volatility.

Forex speculation is the most common form of market participation on a retail level. Investors want to profit like the big banks do. In this case, it's important to make a series of decisions, such as if you want to do the trading yourself, or hire a manager.

1. Self-traded strategy – Client executes his own strategy.

2. Managed Account – Client hires a manager, and pays a fee (usually standard 2/20/20pm)

From that point, you can decide on the type of strategy you feel is most appropriate for you. Forex includes most strategy types we see in other markets, i.e. trend following, fundamental. But Forex has strategy types that are not possible in other markets, such as Latency Arbitrage, Triangular Arbitrage, Multi-Currency Basket, and others.

Although there has been a huge amount of Fraud in retail Forex, still a small group of traders, mostly algorithmic, claims consistent profits. And although some groups have shut down their operations, they did so at a profit. Everyone asks the question, is it possible to make money in Forex? Of course it is, but at what risk?

This well-known Forex group in Boston serves as a reminder for those who know. Infamous Boston Trading and Research (BTR) had 18 months of trading with not a single losing month. That didn't include floating drawdowns, or intra-month drawdowns, but on the surface it looked great. This enabled them to raise a lot of money, and build their book to more than 1,200 customers. Also this was during the 'golden years' before Forex was tainted with fraud associations. BTR really did make a lot of money for clients, and then one day blew up. For reasons unknown, the trader began doubling down his losses and even wiring in more funds to the broker when he received a margin call. Finally this resulted in a near complete wipe out of client capital, more than 90%.

At that point the FBI got involved and raided their offices, as explained by this FBI press release:

In 2007, Karlis and Akyil founded Boston Trading and Research (BTR) and recruited customers to open accounts in order to trade their money in the foreign currency exchange (FOREX) market. By July 2008, BTR had approximately 1,200 customers and more than $35 million under management.

Karlis and Akyil made a series of misrepresentations to customers about how BTR operated and about what they were doing with their money. While they told customers that BTR was compensated based on a percentage of the customers' trading profits, Karlis and Akyil in fact used millions of dollars from BTR customer accounts to pay business expenses, as well as their own personal expenses, such as houses, cars, and jewelry. Karlis and Akyil concealed this misappropriation from BTR's customers on BTR's computerized customer platform and account statements, which, contrary to Karlis and Akyil's representations, did not show all of the trades that BTR had placed using customer money. Karlis and Akyil also told customers that BTR employed strategies to reduce risk, including a protection in the company's computerized trading platform that automatically shut down all trading in a customer's account if BTR's trading lost 30 percent of the value in that account. However, the computerized platform did not have an automatic shut-down mechanism. In fact, over the course of BTR's existence, Akyil repeatedly ignored the 30 percent "draw-down" limits. In August and September 2008, after Karlis had left BTR, Akyil continued trading long after he had lost more than 30 percent of the customer account funds. Ultimately, *this trading caused BTR to lose approximately 90 percent of their customers' money, or more than $30 million*[lxxxii].

The FBI focuses on facts that support the prosecution, leaving out important nuances of BTR's operation. Also, the FBI mischaracterizes BTR as a criminal enterprise. Forex was not regulated in that time. What caused the blow up of BTR was a severe 90% trading loss. Stupid, reckless, but not illegal. Such shades of grey are important to be noticed by would-be Forex investors, Forex students, or anyone interested in Forex.

At the end of the day, the story of BTR is about how not to trade. Probably Akyil fell victim of common psychological issues relating to BTR's perfect track record. This was exacerbated by a huge influx of new client capital, and pressure to perform. The fact that they were not properly regulated, or that Karlis failed to pay his taxes, are not connected to Forex. BTR lost money trading – it was not a Ponzi scheme, or an outright fraud.

But this case presents arguments against both self-trading and managed approaches. BTR was a manager – with a great track record. But Akyil was a trader, who may as well have been trading his own capital.

Managed Accounts – In the case of Managed Accounts, it's important to do extensive due diligence about the program. This should go well beyond normal due diligence. Read the forums, check references, look at the clearing broker and their history, call them directly, and so on. But even after all this which is a lot of work, there are still risks. Even good managers have a bad month, even good managers blow up. But there are FX managed accounts that earn decently year in and year out; month in and month out. They may go through cycles like any program, but they are there. Just be careful, especially in non-regulated jurisdictions, where there are no rules on advertising materials. Typically, established Forex Managers will provide a disclosure document or equivalent which is not much different than a prospectus, as one would receive from a mutual fund. Managers typically charge a management fee, performance fee, and round turn commission.

Self-Traded Accounts – If you want to trade your own Forex account, it's important to decide:

1. What strategy to trade (or a portfolio of strategies)
2. Where the strategy will be executed? (i.e. choose a broker or brokers)

Choosing a good broker can make or break your strategy. Using the MT4 platform as a point of reference, using the same strategy on 30 MT4 brokers will produce 30 different results! Deciding on a broker is as much a personal choice as is deciding on a car. There isn't such thing as 'the best' broker in the world, just as there isn't a 'best' bank. However, a group of 10 – 15 brokers usually dominate the Forex scene, globally. If you are based in the United States, you have few unfortunate choices. Consider expatriating or opening a foreign corporation, for many prudent reasons – not only to open a good Forex account.

Sites such as www.openforexaccount.com operated by Introducing Brokers (IB), provide a list of brokers who will provide decent services. IBs are compensated through the bid/ask spread or via commission. IBs provide different types of value added services, such as reduced trading costs, trading software, or even trading strategies. As a marketing strategy, Elite E Services (EES) would offer clients free Forex algorithms for clients who opened and traded at a broker designated by EES. In this case, EES was compensated through their trading volume only.

A pioneer in this model, EES was a CTA with the CFTC and NFA Member #363609 - and offered clients a unique self-traded environment. Clients could trade on the EESFX ECN powered by ILQ (Institutional Liquidity) and would pay only 5% of the profits per month above a high watermark. This model eliminated the direct costs of trading (whether the bid/ask spread or commission) and allowed clients to profit more than otherwise. It was based on a series of tests where EES discovered that for some high frequency strategies, the commission was greatly impacting profitability. Of course, other IBs didn't like this model as it was 'anti-competitive' and soon after was shut down.

To be prudent, instead of deciding on the best broker, it's wise to choose the top 3 and open 3 accounts in parallel, for means of comparison. And working with an Introducing Broker is always better than not, because the IB does not increase the cost of trading. Brokers do this in order to incentivize clients to use IBs, which offsets some of the workload from the broker directly. The IB will be familiar with broker policies, and be the point of contact with the client. The idea anyway of this is both a marketing model and a sub-contracting model. The IBs are incentivized to drive new business but at the same time, process a lot of the paperwork, and provide customer support for most issues. The range of services provided by IBs varies greatly.

Some IBs such as ATC Brokers[lxxxiii] have gone the extra mile in customization of their technology and Forex offerings, investing even more than the licensed broker (or custodian of funds). Bear in mind this distinction – an IB only 'introduces' business to the FCM/FDM/RFED. But as in this case, trading through one IB versus another – completely changes the trading experience. This can include a difference in commissions, spreads, and/or other order entry features. Some IBs will offer free trading systems, educational materials, or other value added services to customers.

7.2 The Forex Sea of White Labels

An important point of analyses in untangling the Forex Gordian Knot, is the proliferation of Forex white labels. "White Labelling" or "Private Branding" means that a company will use its own label and brand on a 3rd party product or service. In the case of Forex, a broker may 'white label' another broker – so while on your account statements say DBFX on them, you're really trading with FXCM. White Labelling is popular because it protects the value of marketers' brands. Saxo Bank, one of the leading Forex Bank's in the world, claims that more than 90% of its Forex volume comes from white label partners. If such numbers are industry wide, it means that for every 10 brokers out there, 1 is unique and 9 are white labels. There's nothing good or bad about white labels per se, but it should be known and remembered for future Forex reference.

Quality Forex platforms & ECNs barely need to do any marketing at all – the white labels do it for them. Just as there are 1 real product for 9 white labels, such are the numbers for marketers to producers, at least in Forex. Only a small handful of banks & brokerages have developed Forex platforms of any significance.

Because white label data is not published by brokers, we'll never know the full extent of the Forex sea of White Labels. Marketers typically use white labels to protect their investment in marketing. Without the white label, there's no 100% guarantee that they can capture business from broad marketing campaigns. More technically, IBs rely on 'link tracking' to have accounts credited to their IB account – but if a potential customer uses another computer, or goes to the broker directly and opens an account, there's no way for the IB to ever know. Also, white labels often integrate 1 product in their general offering, such as a Securities Broker-Dealer who wants to offer Forex in addition to their existing offering of stocks, options, and related instruments. White labelling is also a quick solution to get started in a new business, while you develop your own platform.

In the case of the Meta Trader 4 platform, configuration settings can create a completely unique trader experience. In some sense, MT4 is a development environment such as Microsoft Windows; more than it is a static platform. That means through the use of configuration settings, customized plugin development, API bridges and other components; brokerages can highly customize their MT4 platform. This makes one MT4 very different from another; and the white label distinguishes this, from a branding perspective. All this configuration is possible without a white label, of course.

Companies offered "Brokerage in a Box" products; an idea pioneered by Elite E Services, Inc. in 2008 – where potential Forex brokers would purchase a complete solution to get started with their own brokerage. This usually included a white labeled trading platform such as MT4, a brokerage license, and a CRM (Customer Relationship Management) tool. Unfortunately, in many cases this was just used to setup fraudulent companies quickly, with the appearance of legitimate Forex brokerages. This practice is less popular today, but beware of brokerages in jurisdictions which are lightly regulated where it is easy to get a brokerage license, such as Cyprus, Seychelles, Mauritius, Belize, and others. It doesn't mean that ALL Forex companies in such places are frauds, it means lightly regulated jurisdictions should be watched closely.

7.3 Who are the winners?

For motivational reasons, we should look at some FX Winners. If you've been reading this book from the beginning, probably you are by now scratching your head or maybe thinking that this "Forex" is more work than its worth, mentally. The fact is that the majority of participants in Forex, both retail and institutional, lose money. This is only due to a lack of knowledge. Forex is not a zero sum game, like the stock market. In Forex, each currency is ever expanding – there is more and more money supply of each currency made every day. By trading Forex, it's possible to capture some of that newly printed money, without having a swap line agreement with the Fed. Let's look at a variety of examples, starting with the most high profile[lxxxiv].

1. George Soros

The British pound shadowed the German mark leading up to the 1990s even though the two countries were very different economically. Germany was the stronger country despite lingering difficulties from reunification, but Britain wanted to keep the value of the pound above 2.7 marks. Attempts to keep to this standard left Britain with high interest rates and equally high inflation, but it demanded a fixed rate of 2.7 marks to a pound as a condition of entering the European Exchange Rate Mechanism (ERM). Many speculators, George Soros chief among them, wondered how long fixed exchange rates could fight market forces, and they began to take up short positions against the pound. Soros borrowed heavily to bet more on a drop in the pound. Britain raised its interest rates to double digits to try to attract investors. The government was hoping to alleviate the selling pressure by creating more buying pressure. Paying out interest costs money, however, and the British government realized that it would lose billions trying to artificially prop up the pound. It withdrew from the ERM and the value of the pound plummeted against the mark. Soros made at least $1 billion off this one trade. For the British government's part, the devaluation of the pound actually helped, as it forced the excess *interest and inflation out of the economy, making it an ideal environment for businesses.*

2. Bill Lipschutz

Born in New York, Bill has always excelled in mathematics and was a bright student overall. He earned a B.A. in Cornell College in Fine Arts and then a Masters degree in Finance back in 1982. Apart from academics, Bill enjoyed reading whatever he could find regarding the stock and Forex market. It is said that during his stay at Cornell, he invested $12000 in stocks, which he turned into $250,000 in only a couple of months, largely thanks to his extensive knowledge of the stock market business. However, he soon lost all his money to stocks due to the erratic nature of the business; after this loss he shifted to a more stable form of trading: the forex. Today, Bill is a well-known forex trader in the financial sector. He is known to have **made over $300 million in a single year from trading on the forex market alone.**

3. John R. Taylor, Jr.

A graduate of Princeton University, John started in the financial sector as a political analyst for Chemical Bank. Just one year into the job, he became the forex analyst for the bank which proved a wonderful opportunity for him to build a network in the foreign exchange world.

FX Concepts was the largest Forex fund in the world, and lasted for 30 years – a very long time in the managed investment world. They were the authority of FX. Clients included the world's most Elite institutions, corporations, governments, and HNWI (High Net worth Individuals). But like all Forex operations, their time was limited, and in 2013 they collapsed[lxxxv]. They had as much as $14 Billion in Assets Under Management (AUM).

But what lessons can be drawn from FX Concepts? Management complacency, a failure to adapt to rapid industry and technological changes and simply wrong-headed bets were the cause of its undoing, said a source with close knowledge of the fund. FX Concepts' management team also failed to adapt quickly enough to changing market conditions; "mission drift" over a number of years rather than too much leverage, the source said. "It was never doubling, tripling or quadrupling up," he said, referring to how much a fund would borrow to invest, much as a house buyer funds a mortgage. The "final straw", according to a Chapter 11 bankruptcy court filing in New York, came in September this year when the San Francisco Employee Retirement System said it was redeeming its investment - 66 percent of FX Concepts' remaining assets.[lxxxvi]

4. Andrew Krieger

*A graduate of the prestigious Wharton Business School at the University of Pennsylvania, Andrew grew to fame when he sold New Zealand currency called Kiwi in between the value of $600 million to about $1 billion which exceeded the money supply in circulation in actuality within New Zealand at that time. Andrew ended up **garnering $300 million in revenue from this transaction alone in 1987 while working at the Bankers Trust.***

SPLITTING PENNIES – *Understanding Forex*

5. James Harris Simons

Although his fund Renaissance mostly trades stocks, he's a pure algorithmic trader, who hires only those with quant backgrounds. James Simons tops the Guinness book of records for the man with the most yearly income; several years, with income in the billions of dollars.[lxxxvii]

For more than two decades, Simons' Renaissance Technologies' hedge funds, which trade in markets around the world, have employed mathematical models to analyze and execute trades, many automated. Renaissance uses computer-based models to predict price changes in financial instruments. These models are based on analyzing as much data as can be gathered, then looking for non-random movements to make predictions.

Of course, these are the only ones we 'know' of – and the reason we know, it is because these traders did this while working for managed funds. They made this money for themselves and for clients. So they were happy to boast about their successful trades after, for marketing reasons, and are now in the financial history books. Others include Stanley Druckenmiller who worked for George Soros, John W. Henry (although Henry primarily traded commodities), Salem Abraham, and many other well-known traders. Currencies are just another market to trade. But with only a few examples such as Soros, their primary market they traded was not currencies. Soros, and his connections with Elite international bankers as pertaining to his Forex trades, are a topic for another book. But it is an interesting unique example, considering his background and later rise to power.

Forex winners typically like to remain anonymous. There are many accounts out there, which have profited 8, 9, and even 10 figures. FX Banks can attest to the fact that although the majority of Forex traders lose, there are a few that win – and win big. Aside from these mentioned, who are they – and where are they?

7.4 D-arb High Frequency Arbitrage in MT4

The decision to include this strategy as an example in this book was well considered. Elite E Services, Inc. (EES) is the corporate author of this book, and the proprietor of this trading strategy "D-arb" – a name we invented that is a contraction of Day – Arbitrage. As the proprietor, there is an obvious lack of objectivity. But the advantage is that EES has first-hand information about this experience. It's a part of our corporate Forex story. We can verify it 100%.

The D-arb strategy is a very simple algorithm with a lot of hard work behind to make it work. This means that months of testing and optimization are required to make this strategy work. That includes optimization of computer hardware & software, strategy parameters, and connection to the bank/broker. It is particular to the broker/bank feed that it works on. Although executed using the MT4 platform, the strategy was using MT4 only as an execution platform, the calculations were done in a custom black box software on the same server as the MT4 platform. D-arb would look for price discrepancies across a plethora of Forex ECNs & banking platforms. What often happens in Forex – when a big order hits the market, it will take a few seconds to reverberate to the other ECNs. For example, if a Swiss fund trading with UBS dumps 5 Billion USD/CHF on the market, it will move the price down, but if the orders go in big chunks, each move may take a few moments to be reflected on the other ECNs. This is not latency arbitrage, although characteristics of the strategy are similar. When d-arb sees an opportunity, it uses maximum leverage to place an order in that direction, and closes it immediately upon achieving its profit goal, usually only 2 or 3 pips but sometimes more. The official average hold time was 1 minute – a lifetime in HFT Forex. But the real arb trades lasted usually 1s – 10s. In fact there was a limitation on the system that it should hold onto trades for at least 1s, as not to arouse suspicion of the counterparties. According to accepted FX trading rules, trading inside of a second can be considered latency arb, and thus 'toxic flow.'

The strategy was originally funded by the EES principal Joseph Gelet and a trading partner and friend, Jordon Grozdanov, with their own capital. After several months of proven success, several select clients were allowed to invest in the program, but with capital restrictions. EES calculated there was a maximum daily profit limitation of about $100,000 - $200,000. Considering the explosive growth functions of the live results, raising money for this strategy didn't seem to be an issue.

In the period from 6/18/2012 until 1/05/2013, on the primary account at ILQ, the strategy generated 2985 trades amounting to a total of $607 Million in volume, making $124,723 in net profit, an absolute return of 1434.4%. Then what happened, the accounts were frozen. This followed by a phone call from an ILQ executive that "This style of trading is not meaningful for the Forex market, we want clients who contribute to Forex in a meaningful way," and "I've been around the block."

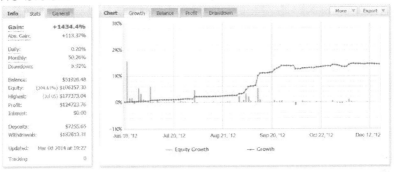

Apparently, they wanted clients that were all losers. EES later learned that other IBs & money managers that were winning consistently, were also stopped. But later, this same firm (ILQ) was heavily fined by the NFA. The NFA complaints make for interesting reading, about the nuances of how a Forex broker works under the guidelines of the NFA[lxxxviii]. In one sentence, ILQ had developed a liquidity pool for smaller orders to 'take the other side' as smaller orders usually lose. This system was so slow and poorly written it couldn't keep up with the fast paced order flow of FX. The most exciting trading day of the d-arb strategy was when the Fed announced operation Twist – September 21, 2011[lxxxix]. This announcement was a real wild card, no one expected it. For a period that lasted several hours, but mostly within 30 minutes of the announcement, there was chaos in the FX markets. Price discrepancies between FX ECNs were huge, and unstable. Spreads widened and inverted. In a period lasting about 20 minutes, the strategy generated 35 trades and gained 7.58%. Profits were exaggerated as in was unique case, the discrepancies were huge. ECNs were off by more than 50 pips in some cases.

Personally, I made more than $14,000 on this strategy, starting with only $1,500 in trading capital, as stated on my 2012 tax return (with some other unrelated trading losses, my net gain for the year in trading profits was about $12,000). The tax professional who assisted me filing my taxes didn't believe it. The point is not the size of the profit which is small, but the percent return, and that it happened because of a Forex algorithm in the United States, and it was all legal, in a regulated environment. There were no 'tricks' or ways to game the system. The profits were withdrawn by check to my bank account. During this whole process, I was an NFA member and CTA registered with the CFTC – 373609. – Joe Gelet

This strategy is no longer viable without significant investment in research & development. But it serves as a great example of the possibilities of Forex for any individual. Of course, such a strategy was developed over a period of years by experienced traders with backgrounds in IT, and much effort was put into its development, testing, and operation. It is unlikely this could be replicated – 'do not try this at home.' **PAST PERFORMANCE DOES NOT GUARANTEE FUTURE RESULTS.** But other systems can be built, the Forex market has changed, there are other opportunities over the Forex horizon, greater and greater by the day. Also, it proves that it IS possible to make money in Forex, on a retail level. Anyone can do it, theoretically.

7.5 Play the Forex Fix - JPY and CHF Pairs Range Bound

This strategy was originally published on Zero Hedge, 11/05/2015xc:

The Forex market is very unusual; it's the largest market in the world with the least amount of significant players (a handful of large banks and central banks control the Forex market). We see every day in the news more and more proof that the Forex market, to a large degree, is fixed. Just today, two traders from Rabobank have been convicted of rigging Libor rates:

Two British citizens face lengthy prison sentences in the US after being convicted of rigging Libor interest rates, in the first case of its kind to reach a courtroom across the Atlantic. The two former traders at the Dutch bank Rabobank - Anthony Allen, Rabobank's former global head of liquidity and finance, and Anthony Conti, a former senior trader - both intend to appeal against the verdicts reached by a federal jury in Manhattan. The US justice department said the verdicts showed that the authorities were determined to crack down on financial crime.

Instead of getting into the detail of how and why the Forex market is different, and that it's fixed; let's look at some charts of USDJPY and EURCHF.

USDJPY 1 Hour

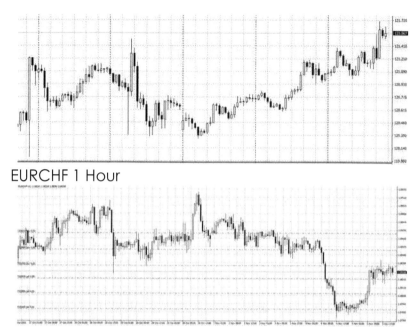

EURCHF 1 Hour

As you can see from the above 2 pairs which are not connected or correlated, there are defined ranges and little direction. While USDJPY has a slight trend up and EURCHF has a slight trend down, they mostly are range bound.

Why is this? Both the BOJ and the SNB have intervened in the market to influence the Forex market, and in some cases have defined predetermined 'fix' levels where they want the currencies to be. They can do that, because they are the primary emission of the currency!

A simple range bound strategy - trade the ranges

If you have the ability to trade spot Forex, trading these ranges is simple. In the case of USDJPY, simply sell when there's a big move up and buy when there's a big move down. There are ways to use algorithms to execute this as well - simply program them to trade against the market - if USDJPY is going up - sell, and if USDJPY is going down, buy. Of course, there are situations where they will break out of the range - which is why it is always prudent to use stop losses and other account protection methods. The ranges certainly will not last forever - but the point is to make money while they last!

Trading ranges with options
If available at your broker, trading these ranges with options is great, especially with options such as 'double no touch' which allows traders to bet that a pair will stay within a certain range. For serious traders, sell a call above the range and sell a put below the range for the duration you believe the range will last (30 days, a reasonable time). Or in the reverse and in the money, buy a put above the range and buy a call below the range.

What this bet is really all about - the Forex Fix

Not only do the banks fix Forex market rates, the central banks openly manipulate the Forex market in many ways:
- Most basically, setting the interest rates
- Capital controls (such as the case with emerging markets)
- Actual Forex market intervention

See a short timeline of central bank intervention from Reuters here.

What are the best range bound Forex pairs?
Simply open your platform and look hourly or daily charts. Currently any CHF pair should be the best, and the best CHF pair - EURCHF. Any pair which is connected to a central bank that openly intervenes in the market, is subject to such behavior. JPY is a little

more volatile than CHF, as Japan has a real economy it needs to manage (no offense, Switzerland!). Remember - Forex is a countertrend market. It always pays in Forex to bet against the trend. Forget "The trend is your friend" and start listening to "Home, home on the range."

7.6 Retire with Rubles

One of the most interesting Forex trades in 2015 was the Russian Ruble. A relatively new currency on the world market (replacing the previous Russian ruble, which replaced the Soviet Ruble), the Russian Ruble started to get attention when Russia butted heads with the United States over the conflict in Ukraine. Starting around September 2014, the Ruble began to slide against the US Dollar and other currencies, fueled by real money flows out of Russia and into G8 currencies, as both Western Corporations with interests in Russia, and Russian oligarchs, sent their money abroad – fearing sanctions, capital controls, or worse. Volatility went 'parabolic' in December 2014, when USD/RUB spiked up more than 25% in one day, and the Central Bank of Russia (CBR) hiked interest rates to 17% from 11%[xci]. [Figure 5 - USD/RUB Daily Chart Sep 2014 - Apr 2015]

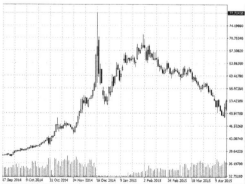

Bank accounts in Russia pay more than 10% in interest in Rubles. The obvious problem, the deteriorating value of the currency. However, this can be mitigated with FX options & FX forwards. A problem for US investors, there isn't any bank/broker who currently offers such contracts. Some US brokers offer trading of the USD/RUB pair with limited leverage, but trading this pair alone wouldn't be enough to passively hedge a cash position in Rubles. Theoretically, what an investor could do, is open a bank account in Russia and hedge the USD/RUB. The best hedge for this circumstance is to purchase forwards. When the investment rolls over, say every year, the investor should rollover the forward contract. The forward will protect against adverse currency movements.

| Swap long | -401.66 |
| Swap short | 52.13 |

The problem with hedging in a spot FX account, is that the account would be continually charged the swap. So this strategy may as well in this case be executed differently; instead of going through all this hassle with bank accounts, simply go short USD/RUB and get the positive swap. But then you'd be suffering pain while the USD/RUB climbs, and without forwards and options, you'd be left playing the waiting game, like traders did who were in the same situation when the JPY carry trade unwound. If USD/RUB really spiked up, your position might be margined out. But without leverage, you should get your 10% a year. So if the USD/RUB goes up less than 10%, you'd be in the money. If USD/RUB went down, you'd have the dual benefit of currency appreciation and interest payment. This is a no-brainer trade for any trader, but certainly is not for the average investor – especially considering the barriers to entry. Only non-US brokers offer a sufficient range of USD/RUB hedging options, and the average investor isn't in a position to easily expatriate or establish a foreign corporation just to trade this strategy. Also, the task of physically visiting Russia to open your bank account requires money, time, visas, and organization. In order to open a bank account in Russia, you must have your passport translated by an official service, and the translation must be notarized. After all this is done and your account is open, then it must be funded in Rubles. You must find a Currency exchange service with reasonable rates, such as Everbank. It will cost 1% - 2% for the hedge, so all this might seem a lot of work for a guaranteed 8%+ return. Some investors would question the safety of funds, but in the case of Sberbank, it's owned by the Russian Government, who is not likely to default in the next 10 years.

Of course, this strategy would apply to any currency offering a decent return, such as used to be the case with the New Zealand Dollar (NZD) around 2000. But as the Fed has ramped up QE, it has convinced other central banks to follow, and the currency wars have ignited in a dramatic race to the bottom.

This is an example of how to make money in Forex. There are literally hundreds of viable strategies that the average investor can execute. If it seems too complex or cumbersome, hundreds of managers offer signals and managed accounts for a reasonable fee. It will take some time for Forex to be accepted as an asset class in the United States as it is in other countries. But meanwhile, the only real barrier to entry is intelligence. With the proliferation of the internet, much quality information can be found online.

The fact is that outside the United States Forex black hole, Forex is seen as both an asset class and a necessary investment market. To some degree, this is because in many countries, there are limited investment options. In Russia, there are hundreds of publicly listed companies, compared to the thousands in the United States. There are tens of thousands of packaged investment products in the United States, ranging from Mutual Funds to Municipal bonds. Many foreign countries, especially emerging markets (EM) do not have such developed investment markets, and so for them, trading Forex is a viable option and even quite common. Perhaps this is another reason why the United States is a Forex black hole. Maybe as traditional investments become less viable, American investors will explore the possibilities in Forex.

7.7 Forex Managed Accounts

From the perspective of the investor, a Forex Managed Account is no different than other types of investments – meaning that investors typically don't understand the nuances of the market. Forex is a traders' market just like stocks, bonds, commodities, and real estate. It's possible to buy and sell Euros and Yen regardless of market direction and make money. But like any market, trading Forex is not easy. However, the advantage of a professional manager, even though it is not a flawless approach, provides many advantages:

- Managers usually have access to exclusive, expensive research & analytics that can assist them in making better decisions
- While managers are incentivized to profit, as the money they are trading is not their completely their own, they typically are more objective
- Managers may have multiple strategies that clients can choose from, offering market diversification
- Sometimes it's possible to customize strategies according to your investment goals, for example if you have a long term long stock position in your portfolio, they may offer a strategy that profits during a market downturn

Currently, Forex Managed Accounts are operated under the jurisdiction of the CFTC (Commodity Futures Trading Commission) policed by the NFA (National Futures Association). The NFA has several categories for Forex Account Managers, most of them are either a CTA (Commodity Trading Advisor) or a CPO (Commodity Pool Operator). A CTA is similar to a CPO but a CTA doesn't accept customer funds directly – they are handled by the clearing broker, usually an FCM (Futures Commissions Merchant) or RFED (Retail Foreign Exchange Dealer). In the case of a CTA, the client opens an account with the registered institution, and signs a LPOA (Limited Power of Attorney) with the CTA, where the details of fees and other nuances are explained. Because a CTA usually trades many customer accounts, they are often grouped into one 'master account' – which the CTA trades as one account. Fees are usually calculated and charged monthly, and the customer can usually revoke the LPOA at any time.

With a CPO, the customer sends funds directly to the manager. CPOs are usually corporations, and sometimes are called 'hedge funds.' CPOs have much more customer liability and accounting as they are the custodian of the funds.

Forex CTA's have special designations that they trade Forex, but from the perspective of the investor, it is transparent – as all he normally would see is a summary profit and loss (P&L) report which includes fees and commissions. What is traded, the underlying, is largely irrelevant to the investor. A Forex CTA can offer multiple strategies, as they usually do.

One such Forex CTA is Fortress Capital, an established Registered Investment Advisor (RIA) and NFA Member, who now offers Forex Managed Accounts. www.fortresscapitalinc.com Fortress Capital is also a Forex Introducing Broker.

Minimum investment amounts in Forex CTAs range from $10,000 to up to $5,000,000 depending on the strategy and the existing AUM (Assets Under Management). However, typically only a fraction of the capital is actually at risk. Although it's possible that a CTA could achieve a 99% drawdown, this is very difficult to do, because most brokers have auto-liquidate functions whereby trades will be closed if they reach certain negative levels, such as 50% equity drawdown on any account. A 20% drawdown in Forex can be considered normal in some circumstances.

Many irregularities exist in the regulations due to the nature of how Forex trades vs. other markets. The rules and regulations were mostly developed for other markets, and in a period where there was no electronic trading. One example is drawdown statistics. An important data point when analyzing any strategy is something called Sharpe Ratio. Sharpe Ratio determines how much money was made with what risk. When evaluating any strategy, it's most important to determine how risky it is, more than the absolute return. Sharpe Ratio is a measure of return divided by the amount of risk used.[xcii]

The point of such analysis is to examine absolute returns, at what cost of risk? Or in other words, how much risk was taken in order to achieve those returns?

This can be tricky, because fraudulent managers and pyramid schemes often have very high Sharpe ratios. In fact, this can be a red flag for a fraud examiner. Some managers will provide Sharpe ratios and some not – but if they provide performance statistics, this can be interpolated.

However, a problem with reporting standards is that only monthly, end of month data is displayed. For example, a manager could theoretically have a 50% loss and recover from it inside of a month, and report 0% for that month. An investor would never know about this extreme situation, according to how the reporting standards in the regulations work. So a monthly performance capsule by itself, is not sufficient information to evaluate a strategy.

However, if a strategy is consistent, has many clients, and respectable AUM, probably the management is decent. A number of factors should be considered outside the performance of any strategy, such as:

- Reputation of the manager, the firm, and related entities.
- Perceived knowledge of the manager, which can be defined by peers. For example, has the manager been published in financial journals? Has the manager been referenced by major news stories? These are all signs of credibility.
- The diversity of the strategies offered. Does the manager rely on a single methodology? (i.e. putting all their eggs in one basket) And if the manager does rely on a simple snazzy method, is there a backup or hedge in place should this method fail?

At the end of the day, it's possible to open multiple managed accounts, so a prudent investor can simply diversify into multiple CTA strategies with a single CTA or with different CTAs. In fact, there are CPOs who only invest in other CPOs. These are called sometimes 'Master Strategies' or in the hedge fund world "Fund of Funds." And the most interesting are the new derivative fund called "F3s" for short, which are "Funds of Funds of Funds" or in plain English, they allocate their investment dollars to Funds of Funds only[xciii].

First there were hedge funds, then there were funds-of-hedge funds, and now, fund-of-fund-of-hedge funds have entered the alternatives space. While less than a dozen or so firms globally offer this type of product, most of them domiciled in Europe, one firm here in the U.S. has created a footprint in the industry with this unusual type of investment vehicle.

Last year, Gregoire Capital, which has trademarked the name F3, broke through what it calls the critical $500 million-mark in assets under management needed to attract institutional investors. It is now managing approximately $800 million in its multi-layered F3 funds, but it isn't stopping there. In January, the firm launched an offshore version of its Tactical Equity Partners fund, which is designed to be a relative-return substitute for mid-cap and small-cap equities in a traditional portfolio with only half of the volatility.

Navigating through the sea of managers and layers of strategies and fees can be intimidating at first, but each manager provides a disclosure document or equivalent that explains all risks and fees, the background of the manager, and the strategies they offer.

Investors are faced with the choice, do your own homework, or trust someone. The problem with trusting someone is that how does one know if they should trust this person, without doing their own homework, thus spending the time to educate themselves anyway? In other words, investors are making decisions, involving making judgements on existing funds. What makes them qualified to do so? Doing your own research and self-education is an obvious precursor. Experience can be expensive, if a bad choice is made. The scariest scenarios such as Madoff, PFG, Amaranth Advisors [xciv], caught even trained and licensed financial professionals. So when evaluating a manager, bear in mind the most important risk – that of insolvency of the custodian, recklessness of the manager, or outright fraud. If these can be avoided, the worst loss an investor could suffer should not be greater than 25% with a few rare exceptions.

Some Forex Managed Accounts will be aggressive, some conservative, and some in between. Some managers will offer the same strategy at an increased leverage, such as "Strategy F66 x2" or 2x which means that capital is traded as if it's twice as much, sometimes referred to as notional capital. This more than doubles the risk, but for sophisticated investors it allows them to grow their capital faster – and they can handle the risk. Even considering all these statements, investors should be prepared to lose 100% of your capital in a Forex Managed Account or any similar investment. Because if you can't afford to lose it, you shouldn't be risking it. Practically, many managers suggest to invest 10% - 20% of your existing portfolio into a Forex Managed Account as a maximum, and only 'risk capital' which means money you can afford to lose.

Forex Managed Accounts are not for everyone! But they do provide a simple way for investors to participate in the Forex markets, and they are similar to other investments (such as commodity managed accounts, and other managed accounts). Risk disclosure disclosure – the beginning of any professional disclosure document will contain several pages of risk disclosures, such as:

THE RISK OF LOSS IN TRADING COMMODITY INTERESTS CAN BE SUBSTANTIAL. YOU SHOULD THEREFORE CAREFULLY CONSIDER WHETHER SUCH TRADING IS SUITABLE FOR YOU IN LIGHT OF YOUR FINANCIAL

CONDITION. IN CONSIDERING WHETHER TO TRADE OR TO AUTHORIZE SOMEONE ELSE TO TRADE FOR YOU, YOU SHOULD BE AWARE OF THE FOLLOWING: IF YOU PURCHASE A COMMODITY OPTION YOU MAY SUSTAIN A TOTAL LOSS OF THE PREMIUM AND OF ALL TRANSACTION COSTS. IF YOU PURCHASE OR SELL A COMMODITY FUTURES CONTRACT OR SELL A COMMODITY OPTION OR ENGAGE IN OFF-EXCHANGE FOREIGN CURRENCY TRADING YOU MAY SUSTAIN A TOTAL LOSS OF THE INITIAL MARGIN FUNDS OR SECURITY DEPOSIT AND ANY ADDITIONAL FUNDS THAT YOU DEPOSIT WITH YOUR BROKER TO ESTABLISH OR MAINTAIN YOUR POSITION. IF THE MARKET MOVES AGAINST YOUR POSITION, YOU MAY BE CALLED UPON BY YOUR BROKER TO DEPOSIT A SUBSTANTIAL AMOUNT OF ADDITIONAL MARGIN FUNDS, ON SHORT NOTICE, IN ORDER TO MAINTAIN YOUR POSITION. IF YOU DO NOT PROVIDE THE REQUESTED FUNDS WITHIN THE PRESCRIBED TIME, YOUR POSITION MAY BE LIQUIDATED AT A LOSS, AND YOU WILL BE LIABLE FOR ANY RESULTING DEFICIT IN YOUR ACCOUNT. UNDER CERTAIN MARKET CONDITIONS, YOU MAY FIND IT DIFFICULT OR IMPOSSIBLE TO LIQUIDATE A POSITION. THIS CAN OCCUR, FOR EXAMPLE, WHEN THE MARKET MAKES A ''LIMIT MOVE.'' THE PLACEMENT OF CONTINGENT ORDERS BY YOU OR YOUR TRADING ADVISOR, SUCH AS A ''STOP-LOSS'' OR ''STOPLIMIT'' ORDER, WILL NOT NECESSARILY LIMIT YOUR LOSSES TO THE INTENDED AMOUNTS, SINCE MARKET CONDITIONS MAY MAKE IT IMPOSSIBLE TO EXECUTE SUCH ORDERS. A ''SPREAD'' POSITION MAY NOT BE LESS RISKY THAN A SIMPLE ''LONG'' OR ''SHORT'' POSITION. THE HIGH DEGREE OF LEVERAGE THAT IS OFTEN OBTAINABLE IN COMMODITY INTEREST TRADING CAN WORK AGAINST

YOU AS WELL AS FOR YOU. THE USE OF LEVERAGE CAN LEAD TO LARGE LOSSES AS WELL AS GAINS. IN SOME CASES, MANAGED COMMODITY ACCOUNTS ARE SUBJECT TO SUBSTANTIAL CHARGES FOR MANAGEMENT AND ADVISORY FEES. IT MAY BE NECESSARY FOR THOSE ACCOUNTS THAT ARE SUBJECT TO THESE CHARGES TO MAKE SUBSTANTIAL TRADING PROFITS TO AVOID DEPLETION OR EXHAUSTION OF THEIR ASSETS. THIS DISCLOSURE DOCUMENT CONTAINS AT PAGES 17, 18 A COMPLETE DESCRIPTION OF EACH FEE TO BE CHARGED TO YOUR ACCOUNT BY THE COMMODITY TRADING ADVISOR. THIS BRIEF STATEMENT CANNOT DISCLOSE ALL THE RISKS AND OTHER SIGNIFICANT ASPECTS OF THE COMMODITY INTEREST MARKETS. YOU SHOULD THEREFORE CAREFULLY STUDY THIS DISCLOSURE DOCUMENT AND COMMODITY INTEREST TRADING BEFORE YOU TRADE, INCLUDING THE DESCRIPTION OF THE PRINCIPAL RISK FACTORS OF THIS INVESTMENT, AT PAGES 12, 13, 14, 15, 16. YOU SHOULD ALSO BE AWARE THAT THIS COMMODITY TRADING ADVISOR MAY ENGAGE IN OFF-EXCHANGE FOREIGN CURRENCY TRADING. SUCH TRADING IS NOT CONDUCTED IN THE INTERBANK MARKET. THE FUNDS DEPOSITED WITH A COUNTERPARTY FOR SUCH TRANSACTIONS WILL NOT RECEIVE THE SAME PROTECTIONS AS FUNDS USED TO MARGIN OR GUARANTEE EXCHANGE-TRADED FUTURES AND OPTION CONTRACTS. IF THE COUNTERPARTY BECOMES INSOLVENT AND YOU HAVE A CLAIM FOR AMOUNTS DEPOSITED OR PROFITS EARNED ON TRANSACTIONS WITH THE COUNTERPARTY, YOUR CLAIM MAY NOT BE TREATED AS A COMMODITY CUSTOMER CLAIM FOR PURPOSES OF SUBCHAPTER IV OF CHAPTER 7 OF THE BANKRUPTCY CODE AND REGULATIONS THEREUNDER.

YOU MAY BE A GENERAL CREDITOR AND YOUR CLAIM MAY BE PAID, ALONG WITH THE CLAIMS OF OTHER GENERAL CREDITORS, FROM ANY MONIES STILL AVAILABLE AFTER PRIORITY CLAIMS ARE PAID. EVEN FUNDS THAT THE COUNTERPARTY KEEPS SEPARATE FROM ITS OWN FUNDS MAY NOT BE SAFE FROM THE CLAIMS OF PRIORITY AND OTHER GENERAL CREDITORS. THE RISK OF LOSS IN TRADING OVER THE COUNTER SPOT FOREIGN EXCHANGE (FOREX) CAN BE SUBSTANTIAL. YOU SHOULD THEREFORE CAREFULLY CONSIDER WHETHER SUCH TRADING IS SUITABLE FOR YOU IN LIGHT OF YOUR FINANCIAL CONDITION. THE HIGH DEGREE OF LEVERAGE THAT IS OFTEN OBTAINABLE IN FOREX TRADING CAN WORK AGAINST YOU AS WELL AS FOR YOU. THE USE OF LEVERAGE CAN LEAD TO LARGE LOSSES AS WELL AS GAINS. PAST RESULTS ARE NOT INDICATIVE OF FUTURE RESULTS. (THE CTA) cannot and does not guarantee the accuracy, validity, timeliness, or completeness of any performance information or data obtained from third parties and made available to you or reviewed and relied upon by you for any particular purpose. In particular, (THE CTA) does not stand behind nor can it vouch for or verify any of the performance statistics that you will view on any websites that you may land on or link to from (THE CTA) website, or that recommend or link to. FURTHER, YOU SHOULD CAREFULLY REVIEW THE INFORMATION CONTAINED IN THE RISK DISCLOSURE STATEMENT OF THE FUTURES COMMISSION MERCHANT OR RETAIL FOREIGN EXCHANGE DEALER THAT YOU SELECT TO CARRY YOUR ACCOUNT. THIS COMMODITY TRADING ADVISOR IS PROHIBITED BY LAW FROM ACCEPTING FUNDS IN THE TRADING ADVISOR'S NAME FROM A CLIENT FOR TRADING COMMODITY INTERESTS. YOU MUST PLACE

ALL FUNDS FOR TRADING IN THIS TRADING PROGRAM DIRECTLY WITH A FUTURES COMMISSION MERCHANT OR RETAIL FOREIGN EXCHANGE DEALER, AS APPLICABLE.

After one reads this for the first time, one may ask the question – does anyone actually invest in this? It seems shocking, to read such information (before even knowing what the investment is, or other information). The fact is though, it's simply because it is regulation at work. The NFA is a self-regulatory body, and over time, frauds become less and less. Forex being a new game in town, saw an initial spike in fraud and lower and lower every year. It's because of such disclaimers, and policing by the regulators. Although there were many unintended consequences of the Dodd-Frank regulations, the regulators generally speaking did crack down on Forex related fraud, which is today almost non-existent. Such disclaimers are required by law and regulation. So, the problem is not such disclaimers and disclosures in disclosure documents and prospectus, the problem is that such disclosures are not required before you use the Forex Banking Money system. In fact, such disclaimers should also be included before you use the US Dollar, such as:

WARNING – THE VALUE OF THE DOLLAR WILL DETERIORATE SLOWLY OVER TIME. BECAUSE THIS DETERIORATION HAPPENS SO SLOWLY, SO SUBTLY, YOU ARE NOT LIKELY TO NOTICE. EACH YEAR, EVEN WITH INTEREST PAYMENTS, THE MONEY IN YOUR BANK ACCOUNT, SAVINGS ACCOUNT, OR MONEY MARKET ACCOUNT, WILL BUY LESS AND LESS. IT MAY BE NECESSARY FOR INVESTORS TO TAKE HIGH RISKS IN ORDER TO KEEP UP WITH INFLATION AND THE RAPID

RATE OF DETERIORATION OF THE US DOLLAR. THERE ARE NO GUARANTEES WHAT THE FED WILL DO, SUCH AS AN EMERGENCY RATE DECREASE, PRINTING OF TRILLIONS OF DOLLARS, AND OTHER MEASURES THAT CAN CAUSE THE US DOLLAR TO RAPIDLY LOSE ITS VALUE. THE MONEY YOU HAVE NOW IN YOUR ACCOUNT IS WORTH LESS AND LESS EACH DAY. THE INTEREST THAT YOU MAY BE PAID TO KEEP YOUR MONEY IN A BANK, IF ANY, WILL CERTAINLY NOT KEEP UP WITH THE RATE OF INFLATION. IN FACT, IT IS GUARANTEED THAT ANY GUARANTEED INVESTMENT SUCH AS BONDS, MONEY MARKET ACCOUNTS, AND OTHERS WILL PROVIDE ONLY A RETURN OF YOUR MONEY, NOT A RETURN ON YOUR MONEY. HOWEVER ONE CALCULATES INFLATION, INCLUDING FOOD, ENERGY, AND THINGS THAT USERS WILL ACTUALLY SPEND THEIR MONEY ON, IT'S MUCH GREATER THAN 2% PER YEAR. IT CAN BE AS HIGH AS 10% OR EVEN GREATER. BY COMMITTING YOUR US DOLLARS TO A LONG TERM GUARANTEED INVESTMENT, YOU ARE GUARANTEEING THAT YOU WILL GET YOUR MONEY BACK, BUT IT WILL BE WORTH LESS IN ABSOLUTE VALUE TERMS THAN IT IS TODAY. BE ADVISED THAT IF YOU DO CHOOSE TO DO YOUR OWN INVESTING, THERE IS A STEEP LEARNING CURVE AND THERE ARE MANY DANGERS AND PITFALLS. BEATING REAL INFLATION IN THE US DOLLAR ENVIRONMENT IS AN EXTREMELY COMPLICATED GAME. YOU WILL BE COMPETING WITH THE SMARTEST, MOST WELL FUNDED GROUPS IN THE WORLD. THEIR GOAL IS NOT ONLY TO GROW THEIR PORTFOLIOS AND BEAT INFLATION, BUT TO MAKE SURE THAT YOURS GROWS SLOWER THAN THEIRS, AS IT IS A GAME OF MUSICAL CHAIRS, AND IN ORDER FOR THEM TO SUCCEED, THEY NEED YOU TO BE WITHOUT A CHAIR WHEN THE MUSIC

STOPS. SYSTEMICALLY SPEAKING, BECAUSE WE HAVE A DEBT BASED MONEY SYSTEM, THE ONLY WAY FOR THESE WELL TRAINED SHARKS TO WIN IS FOR OTHERS TO LOSE. THEY MAY NOT UNDERSTAND THIS CONSCIOUSLY, BUT LOOKING AT MARKET DATA WE CAN SEE THAT THE MAJORITY OF INVESTORS ARE FLEECED NEARLY EVERY 10 YEARS, THROUGH AN ENGINEERED CRASH OF VARIOUS KINDS – SUCH AS THE .COM CRASH, 1987 STOCK MARKET CRASH, 2007 REAL ESTATE / SUBPRIME CRASH, AND OTHER FINANCIAL CALAMATIES THAT ARE DESIGNED SPECIFICALLY TO MAKE THE RICH VERY RICH AND WIPE OUT ANY SAVERS AND PRUDENT WORKING PEOPLE TRYING TO STAY AHEAD OF INFLATION WITH THEIR 401K. IN ORDER TO COMPETE IN THIS GAME, A PHD FROM PRINCETON WILL NOT EVEN GUARANTEE YOUR SUCCESS, BUT IT CAN SIGNIFICANTLY HELP, AS WELL AS HELP UNDERSTANDING THE FUTILITY OF SAVING AND HOW THE MARKET IS DESIGNED AS BOOM AND BUST BECAUSE OF THE DEBT BASED MONEY SYSTEM. BY PARTICIPATING IN THE US DOLLAR SYSTEM, BY KEEPING US DOLLARS IN ANY SIGNIFICANT QUANTITY, YOU ARE AGREEING TO BEAR THE BURDEN OF RISKS ASSOCIATED WITH THE CURRENT FIAT DEBT BASED US DOLLAR SYSTEM, AND OPENING YOURSELF UP TO SITUATIONS SUCH AS A RUN ON THE US DOLLAR, COLLAPSE OF THE US DOLLAR, DEFAULT ON THE US DOLLAR, AND OTHER CIRCUMSTANCES WHICH COULD POTENTIALLY MAKE YOUR US DOLLARS COMPLETELY WORTHLESS.

Of course, if this was explained to people at the local retail branch of your savings and loan bank, probably very few people would keep the majority of their hard earned money in a savings or money market account.

It has happened before – it can happen again. In fact – we are more at risk now than during previous times, due to the internet and electronic markets. It happened in 2007 – but the market was saved. The point is – the Forex system is relatively stable but with periods of extreme volatility. A few times, the system was very close to the brink of collapse. This should be explained to investors who keep the majority of their savings in US Dollars!

8: Forex Computing

Reading the news, Forex may sound exotic, thrilling, exciting; something from a James Bond novel. But the reality, Forex is hard computer work. As the Forex market is completely artificial, the only reality of Forex exists inside the computer. It's important to have a strong understanding of computing and mathematics to fully understand Forex. Forex companies and banks use their slightly higher math skills to profit from customers.

Unfortunately, those who designed the Forex market had not computer backgrounds, nor computers in mind. Forex is very mathematically simple, even with strange rules such as 2 day settlement, and non-base pairs.

During the period when Forex grew from nothing into the global powerhouse of trade that it is today, so did the Personal Computer (PC) and the internet. This also coincided with the downturn and demise of mainframe computing, ironically even with the big banks who were IBMs best customers during the prime time of mainframe systems. Still, IBM plays a critical role in banking computing with mainframes such as their IBM System Z^{xcv}.

So while the majority of banking functions are running on a stable mainframe IBM, the global Forex system was haphazardly patched together as if with duct tape, held together by desire to trade only. Forex uses a client-server model, whereby the bank/broker usually operates a small datacenter or rents a suite in NY4, and the client connects via their desktop PC through a client software, usually Microsoft based. Still a number of Forex orders are done by voice. In 2008, one of the top 10 Forex banks didn't have an electronic platform AT ALL. Few standards existed, banks bought the best servers on the market, similar to what was used by hedge funds for the growing 'quant' strategies. Forex was born into a world with explosive computer growth, coinciding with an increase in internet bandwidth. There was electronic trading in the 80's, but it was often proprietary bank to bank connections, and often a combination of electronic and voice confirmation. As the internet only existed in select institutions and was not widely proliferated, multiple peer to peer connections that are today common were not possible, and latency was significant. Forex dealers would literally keep other dealers on the phone on multiple phone lines in order to keep real-time lines of communication between major Forex trading centers such as London, Tokyo, New York, and others.

8.1 FIX API – Fix Protocol
Finally, in 1992 the Fix Protocol was developed, and eagerly adopted by banks to trade the Forex[xcvi]. This system is currently the dominating system used today for 99% of Forex trading, although FIX will usually connect to a 'front end' trading system such as Meta Trader, CTrader, AxiTrader, Bloomberg Terminal, Currenex, or other.

*The **Financial Information eXchange (FIX)** protocol is an electronic communications protocol initiated in 1992 for international real-time exchange of information related to the securities transactions and markets. With trillions of dollars traded annually on the*

NASDAQ alone, financial service entities are investing heavily in optimizing electronic trading and employing direct market access (DMA) to increase their speed to financial markets. Managing the delivery of trading applications and keeping latency low increasingly requires an understanding of the FIX protocol.

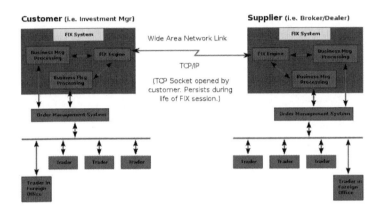

FIX gives traders the flexibility to program their own instructions directly to the FIX API of their counterparty, or to setup a 'bridge' to another system, such as a front end system. FIX requires a FIX engine, which runs FIX commands in real time. FIX is now the international standard for Forex trading. Although FIX is open source, and completely royalty free, many vendors have optimized and rewritten code to work with FIX, which is for sale commercially. FIX engines can range from $10,000 - $100,000 including plugins and various adapters. Many free open source FIX engines are available online, such as the popular Quick FIX www.quickfixengine.org.

8.2 Forex algorithms

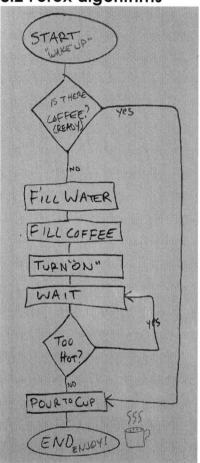

What is an algorithm, commonly referred to as 'algo?' Let's demystify what this is, by use of the most basic algorithm used by scientists; classification and identification. An algorithm is not connected to computers per se. **An algorithm is a process; a series of steps.** (Berlinski, 2001) Algorithms always have a beginning and an end. An algorithm can describe making the morning pot of coffee, as follows:

1. Wake up! (Start)

2. Question: Is there fresh coffee? If yes, proceed to step 7. If no, go to step 3.
3. Pour water into reservoir.
4. Open can of coffee, pour coffee into tray.
5. *(optional step) Wash coffee pot, if necessary.*
6. Turn on machine, and wait.
7. Pour coffee into coffee cup.
8. *(optional step) Add sugar or milk as needed.*
9. Enjoy! (End)

This simple algorithm is one everyone can relate to, as almost all human beings have at some point in their life, made a pot of coffee. Forex algorithms are no different – they are a series of steps that programmers use to develop automated trading robots. There is a big myth about algorithmic trading that some intelligence is involved. In fact, 99% of algorithms are developed based on human instruction – not machine intelligence! That means algorithmic trading is a means of speedy and efficient execution, nothing more. The algorithms do not 'decide' anything – they do what the programmer tells them. There are obvious efficiencies and speed advantages with this method. Another myth - that algorithms were somehow to blame for the flash crash, and for a number of market hiccups. Algorithms, computers don't make mistakes – programmers do! Faulty programming and failure to sufficiently test and implement and quality any program can result in strange behavior, system malfunction, or complete crash.

Because of the complexities of Forex trading as an investment strategy, and the fact that the market is practically always open, this led to the development of Forex algorithms as a means of execution, both on the buy side and on the sell side. Buy Side and Sell Side, this is securities lingo – the sell side is the underwriter / issuer of the security, the buy side are the investors.

Forex is unique in this mathematically, compared to all other markets – stocks, bonds, commodities, and others. In Forex, you must trade one currency for another. You cannot just 'buy Dollars' – it must be against another currency. The pair trading system can confuse first time traders, as the math is unique. The most basic example, EUR/USD 1.20 – means that 1 Euro = 1.20 US Dollars.

Unlike other markets, Forex accounts must choose their base pair. Many banks will offer choices, while in the US accounts are pretty much all USD base. Profit & Loss (P&L) is always first calculated in the pair base and then translated to the account base. This can tricky and even a source of revenue for brokers. For same pair – account base, calculation is easy. If for example we use a US Dollar base account, and trade in EUR/USD 10,000 contract, the P/L is $1 per pip. P/L will fluctuate by the $1 in multiples of $1. When the position is closed, the exact amount is credited or debited to the account balance. This is not the case when a pair is traded with a different pair base – such as EUR/GBP. In the case of EUR/GBP, profit will be in GBP. So when the EUR/GBP position is closed, the profit in GBP will need to be converted to USD before being credited or debited from the account balance. This is where Forex brokers can make a lot of money – because who checks the conversion of profits to base currencies? And who cares – the amounts are very small. On a $100 profit, the translation fee could be $1 or $2 – a huge spread. But not much as a % of a single trade profit (in the minds of many traders). To show the extremity of this, the average industry standard spread on EUR/USD is 1 pip. A 1% spread would represent about 100 pips, or 100 times greater! If a spot trader saw a spread of 100 pips in a dealing platform, they would cry foul. But it happens all the time in the translations of non-base currency profits, and few notice. But anyway, there's little a trader can do about it, anyway.

Because of this, many banks / brokers will publish these rates, with explanations of how they do this. Another similar instance of such practices involves rollover / swap spreads – brokers can widen them for a little extra profit. But this is less severe, especially now with the near zero interest rate environment in major currencies. But for example, if we were to launch a strategy that depended on interest swap payments, it would be prudent to compare potential counterparties solely based on their swap spreads, rollover payment terms, and related info.

Forex algorithms take many forms. Algorithmic traders each believe their own algorithm is the only proper way to trade. But overall, the majority of algorithmic traders win, compared to non-algorithmic traders.

Meta Trader 4 has become the global standard in Forex algorithm development. It is because MT4 is available free from hundreds of Forex brokers. As of this writing there are rumored to be 2,000 MT4 brokers in the world with full licenses, and an unknown number of white labels. MT4 provides developers with a sandbox for developing, testing, implementing, and qualifying new strategy ideas, without the normal costs involved.   On par with traditional software development, to develop a Forex algorithm properly, the costs range from $50,000 - $200,000 including all necessary hardware, software, and development tools.

Many strategies developed by hobbyists and professional programmers in their spare time have become popular due to their cost (usually free), ease of use, and support.   Although this loose knit community of developers, traders, and marketers is not completely professional (such as a trade organization), it has been very healthy for the development of Forex algorithms and for algorithms generally.   The High Level Language (HLL) or 'script language' provided by Meta Quotes "MQL" gives programmers the ability to quickly code strategies and test them in the market on a paper account or a live account with small amount of money. It is also easy to learn this language for anyone with a computer background or who has the time to learn.

The other advantage of this platform is that it provides somewhat of a standard. A developer who makes an algorithm in MQL can trade their Expert Advisor (EA) at any Forex broker who offers this platform. So if the broker provides a poor level of service, the trader can simply close his account and use the EA elsewhere. This is in contrast to a FIX/API environment which is very bank/broker specific, meaning any dispute with the counterparty means the trader needs to completely rebuild his strategy from the ground up. This puts MT4 brokers in a situation to heavily compete for client business, at least outside of the heavily regulated United States. MT4 brokers will provide clients with a huge amount of value added services to gain this profitable business. Algorithms trade actively and produce a lot of volume with no risk to the broker.

Forex brokers will provide the free use of their own VPS (Virtual Private Server) sometimes located in the same datacenter as their trading server, tools and indicators, and even free custom programming of Forex algorithms, if a customer will choose them. Spreads have gone to near zero, with brokers relying on huge account turnovers to compensate. As the industry grows in the medium term, brokers will attempt to seize profits from profitable systems, as the competition will drive commissions to almost nothing.

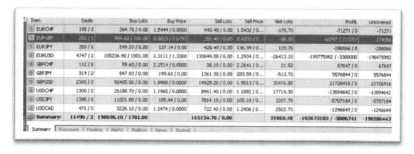

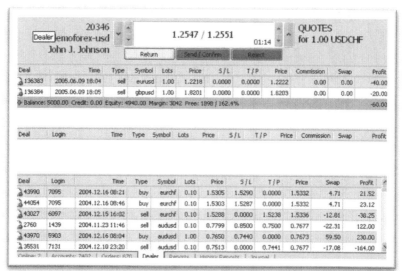

While screenshots of the Meta Trader 4 (MT4) client terminal are proliferated everywhere, not so widely seen are the screenshots of the 'backend' dealing system. Just as clients see a quote window displaying buy/sell rates of Forex pairs, the dealers see a similar window – but instead of Forex pairs, they see clients' orders and requests for quotes. They see in fact, much more information than the client sees; they see the market, but they also see the combination of all customer orders. If the broker is sizeable, this can show dealers the client sentiment (for example, customers will have a net position long or short Euro).

Some brokers such as Oanda publish this information as a tool to assist traders[xcvii]. In the below image, they display open positions as long/short ratios. In the example of EUR/USD below, 49.25% of all customer positions in Oanda in EUR/USD are long, and 50.75% are short. This is similar to the dataset COT (Commitment of Traders) provided for the commodity markets [xcviii]. Although the huge difference, in the Forex market – the customers of Oanda are not likely to affect market price, such as the case in the commodity markets of which 100% of customer positions are known. Oanda represents only a fraction of a fraction of global FX volume, so even if long/short ratios were extreme, it wouldn't likely trigger a price spike. However, many believe that such indication is statistically significant because of the large size of the sample; Oanda has a huge customer base, some of whom are institutional traders. So even though the data only represents a tiny fraction of a fraction of a market, so the thinking goes, the rest of the market is of the same sentiment, or similar.

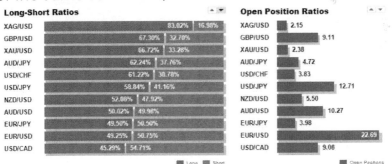

The reason for the lengthy elaboration of Forex brokers here regarding the topic of algorithms, because the Forex broker exactly determines the style, shape, and ultimately the success of any Forex algorithm. In many cases, the bank/broker environment can make or break an algorithm. In other cases, sub-routines or sub-algorithms need to be developed just as a means of execution of the master strategy.

Most Forex algorithms contain several main components:

- Environment variables
- Parameters / Settings
- Execution model - Runtime
- Debugging

In most cases, the actual strategy itself can be very simple. In the most basic example, a moving average crossover triggers a buy or sell. Most commonly, the fast line crosses over the slow line, generating a sell signal – and a buy signal for the opposite:

In the above photo, a buy signal is generated when the fast line in blue (MA 5) crosses under the slow line in red (MA 30). A Sell signal is generated when the red line crosses over the slow line. As the technical theory goes, this is a sign of an increase or decrease in momentum.

This logic can be programmed into a functional strategy that auto-executes based on these instructions. Other parameters, such as to only trade during certain times, money management rules, are usually left open for the trader to input parameters before execution. For example, the strategy may calculate the size of the trade based on a percent of the account balance, or as a static, predefined size the trader will enter. Such a system then can be used in a variety of ways, depending on the settings used, and underlying instrument used. The same strategy in Forex, can theoretically be used on any pair. However, most strategies will perform better on certain pairs, due to the behavior of the price. The MT4 platform allows the easy testing on all pairs or ones that are chosen, within a reasonable amount of time. The back tester is not very accurate, but it provides a general idea of how the strategy would have done in the past. By improving MT4's native functions, such as by providing precise tick data and spread data, it's possible to use MT4 to create near perfect back test results. If you want to start using Forex algorithms, Meta Trader is the best place to start. Not only it has the best tools and resources for new traders, there is a vast online community of developers, support personnel, and tools that have been developed for a wide range of functions.

Developing a Forex algorithm can be as easy as:

Buy 1 lot EUR/USD at 4:00 pm EST, Close position at 5:30 pm EST.

Forex contracts are usually calculated in lots, 1 lot is 100,000 units of the underlying; 10 lots is 1 million, and so on. Retail brokers offer 'mini lots' which are 10,000 and some brokers offer the ability to trade a single unit! Because volatility of currencies is relatively low, traders usually employ a large degree of leverage. In the United States Forex leverage is capped at 50:1, whereas offshore traders can enjoy up to 500:1 leverage.

In the stock world, trading strategies are categorized into several types such as:

- Discretionary Trading
- Technical / Systemic Trading

Discretionary trading is when the trader decides based on his or her discretion what the market will do. This can be very dangerous even for experienced traders, because humans are subject to emotions and other psychological factors that can negatively influence decision making. Even a trained analyst that adheres to a successful analysis doctrine, over a long period of time, can be worn down by various life factors, stress, fatigue, or just simply have a bad day. Humans are subject to gamblers ruin[xcix]:

- *The original meaning is that a gambler who raises his bet to a fixed fraction of bankroll when he wins, but does not reduce it when he loses, will eventually go broke, even if he has a positive expected value on each bet.*

- *Another common meaning is that a gambler with finite wealth, playing a fair game (that is, each bet has expected value zero to both sides) will eventually go broke against an opponent with infinite wealth. Such a situation can be modeled by a random walk on the real number line. In that context it is provable that the agent will return to his point of origin or go broke and is ruined an infinite number of times if the random walk continues forever.*

For these reasons, most Forex traders want to be system traders, or algorithmic traders. That doesn't mean necessarily having software robots to do your trading for you, it simply means employing a system and following it; i.e. 'system trading.' Of course, the easiest method of system execution, is by automated software robot. But even in that case, the Forex algorithm is not 100% automatic – the trader needs to load the robot, choose the settings, lot size, and pair. For this reason, the same Forex algorithm used by 100 traders can have 100 different results. So Forex algorithms are overall healthy for the Forex market.

With technical or system trading, a method is developed and followed explicitly, with no exceptions. Usually, a 'signal' will determine when a trade is placed, based on predefined mathematical criteria. Some services offer such 'signals' without the full algorithm, whereby the trader will decide to use this 'signal' to place a trade, or not.

While algorithmic trading represents the greater majority of Forex volume, these algorithms are not making 'decisions' on their own, they are only following the rules as programmed by their developers. Usually they are monitored by the developers, who then can use real-time information to optimize the strategy.

Most algorithms require regular optimization in order to succeed in the long term. This is due to market changes. Just because an algorithm is effective during a certain period, does not mean it will continue to be so. However, a properly designed algorithm can be continually optimized, even in real time. Some developers have attempted to develop methods for 'self-optimization' which is near artificial intelligence. But still most algorithms rely on static rules, and settings are optimized only.

8.3 How to develop an algorithm / Forex system strategy

Developing a Forex strategy is akin to developing any strategy. Often in trading, the military is used as a Metaphor. One of the most popular doctrines, Sun Tzu. It is because this ancient war general developed an intelligence doctrine covering all possible situations and circumstances. These were before science – it was ancient game theory. The more recent and Western of such doctrines currently studied at Military Academies comes from Carl von Clausewitz[c]. Game theory provides a more modern framework and more practical examples for strategy development[ci].

Game theory is "the study of mathematical models of conflict and cooperation between intelligent rational decision-makers."[11] Game theory is mainly used in economics, political science, and psychology, as well as logic, computer science, biology and poker.[2] Originally, it addressed zero-sum games, in which one person's gains result in losses for the other participants. Today, game theory applies to a wide range of behavioral relations, and is now an umbrella term for the science of logical decision making in humans, animals, and computers. Modern game theory began with the idea regarding the existence of mixed-strategy equilibria in two-person zero-sum games and its proof by John von Neumann. Von Neumann's original proof used Brouwer fixed-point theorem on continuous mappings into compact convex sets, which became a standard method in game theory and mathematical economics. His paper was followed by the 1944 book Theory of Games and Economic Behavior, co-written with Oskar Morgenstern, which considered cooperative games of several players. The second edition of this book provided an axiomatic theory of expected utility, which allowed mathematical statisticians and economists to treat decision-making under uncertainty.

Forex, as it pertains to strategy development, is a game. So in this context, the user can use any game which is familiar to the user, as a method of reference. Because all of us have at some point in our lives, played a game. So use the game which is most known to you, as the example. Any game involves a series of steps: **1) learning the rules 2) practicing and developing a strategy 3) playing the game 4) improving your strategy.**

In this game analogy, step 4 is the process we recently discussed called 'optimization.' When developing a

Forex strategy, the first step is to decide on a Forex doctrine, or approach to the market. Some example Forex doctrines:

- Forex markets will exactly reflect the underlying fundamentals of the economy supporting the currency, plus the interest rate of the currency (Fundamental / Interest Rate Parity Theory)
- Regional Forex markets have network delays that will create small market price discrepancies, which can be captured (latency arbitrage)
- Due to the overwhelming complexities of "Supercurrencies" – pressure will exert itself driving the value of such currencies down. (Doctrine) The Euro will break up into regional currencies, therefore the Euro will go down (Strategy). We will sell into any Euro strength and build large short position in Euro across a wide variety of currencies (Tactical).

Based on the underlying Doctrine, one should then make a "Trading Plan" which is a business plan outlining how your strategy will be executed.

One method that is popular among quantitative traders, is to perform data analysis of past data. Statistical analysis can find patterns, as simple as EUR/USD increase every Sunday at 6pm EST, and as complex as you can imagine. In a more basic, casual form – traders look at charts and look for patterns. This can be very deceiving though, but any such idea can quickly be tested with automated tools.

In fact, a 'trading plan' is a Forex algorithm. In the case of many strategies, it may not be possible to code them into an automatic system that executes on autopilot. But a trading plan serves the same purpose.

8.4 Forex derivatives

As Forex is a completely artificial market, it's easy to make derivatives. The most basic Forex derivatives:

- Options on currencies pairs
- Forex Futures
- Forwards
- Forex ETFs
- Forex Swaps
- Multi-Currency Debt Swaps
- Binary Options

Options on currencies are not much different than Futures or Stocks; a vanilla option is the right but not the obligation to purchase the underlying currency pair at the expiration date. Some Forex brokers have developed specific Forex options such as 'double no touch' which allows traders to bet on a range.

Forex Futures are popular with hedge funds, because they can trade the EUR/USD as futures such as EC contract [cii] .   Futures have many advantages for institutions over spot Forex, such as:

- A price that tracks the underlying so precisely, it's just like trading Spot FX
- Standardized contract sizes, as all futures have
- The ability to trade EC in your futures account, along with any other futures contract
- Trading on US Soil, on US regulated exchanges

Forwards are unique to Forex. They are very similar to futures. With Forwards, the purchaser agrees to buy the underlying currency, at a particular price, at some date in the future. The price is calculated based on the market, and usually includes some interest rate component. For example, in the case where a currency costs money to hold, such as having a negative swap value, this will be reflected in the Forward price. Theoretically, Forwards are an indication of what the market will be in 3 months, 6 months, and so on. While this is almost never the case, they do provide hedgers with a clear method of managing their risk. Because with Forwards, regardless of the fluctuation, you are guaranteed delivery of your needed currency at the given future date.

Forex ETFs (Exchange Traded Funds) are ETFs which either a currency directly, or a basket of currencies, or with an added component of leverage. An interesting example is UUP[ciii] (US Dollar Index Bullish):

Power Shares DB US Dollar Index Bullish Fund (the Fund) is a separate series of Power Shares DB US Dollar Index Trust (the Trust). The Fund establishes long positions in certain futures contracts (the DX Contracts) with a view to tracking the change Bank Long US Dollar Index (USDX) Futures Index Excess Return (the Index), over time. The Fund seeks to track the Index by establishing long positions in DX Contracts accordingly. The Fund offers common units of beneficial interest (the Shares) only to certain eligible financial institutions (the Authorized Participants) in one or more blocks of 200,000 Shares, called a Basket. The proceeds from the offering of Shares are invested in the Fund. The Fund is managed by DB Commodity Services LLC. The Bank of New York Mellon acts as the administrator of the Fund.

There are many such Forex ETFs that offer stock investors the opportunity to participate in the currency markets. ETFs do not offer leverage and have high costs. However, if a stock fund only has the ability to trade stocks, and they believe McDonalds (MCD) will be negatively impacted by the rising US Dollar, they could go long the US Dollar in their stock account and theoretically anyway, offset the losses of the stock with their profits from the Forex ETF.

Forex Swaps are an agreement to 'swap' one currency for another. The difference between a swap and a normal transaction, a swap happens outside of the market, so it does not affect the market price. Swaps are mostly used by central banks, but not exclusively. Banks create complex derivatives including Forex swap components. An entire library could be written about the world of Forex swap derivatives, because each one is mathematically unique. One option that is easy to understand is barrier options; that are executed when the underlying price reaches a certain barrier (i.e. EUR/USD above 1.3000).

A knock-out option belongs to a class of exotic options – options that have more complex features than plain-vanilla options – known as barrier options. Barrier options are options that either come into existence or cease to exist when the price of the underlying asset reaches or breaches a pre-defined price level within a defined period of time. Knock-in options come into existence when the price of the underlying asset reaches or breaches a specific price level, while knock-out options cease to exist (i.e. they are knocked out) when the asset price reaches or breaches a price level. The basic rationale for using these types of options is to lower the cost of hedging or speculation.[civ]

Down-and-out forex option example

A German exporter wants to hedge US$10 million of export receivables using knock-out put options. The exporter is concerned about a potential strengthening of the Euro (which would mean significantly less Euros when the U.S. dollar receivable is sold), which is currently trading in the spot market at US$ 1 = € 1.1000. The exporter therefore buys a USD put option expiring in one month (with a notional value of US$10 million) that has a strike price of US$ 1 = € 1.0900 and a knock-out barrier of US$ 1 = € 1.0800. The cost of this knock-out put is 50 pips, or € 50,000.

The exporter is speculating that even if the Euro strengthens, it will not do so much past the 1.0900 level. Over the one-month life of the option, if the US$ ever trades below the barrier price of € 1.0800, it will be knocked out and cease to exist. It only needs to tick below this price, for one tick (not stay there). But if the US$ does not trade below US$1.0800, the exporter's profit or loss depends on the exchange rate shortly before (or at) option expiration.

Assuming the barrier has not been breached, three potential scenarios arise at or shortly before option expiration –

(1) The U.S. dollar is trading between € 1.0900 and € 1.0800. In this case, the gross profit on the option trade is equal to the difference between 1.0900 and the spot rate, with the net profit equal to this amount less 50 pips.

Assume the spot rate just before option expiration is 1.0810. Since the put option is in-the-money, the exporter's profit is equal to the strike price of 1.0900 less the spot price (1.0810), less the premium paid of 50 pips. This is equal to 90 – 50 = 40 pips = $40,000.

Here's the logic. Since the option is in-the-money, the exporter sells US$10 million at the strike price of 1.0900, for proceeds of €10.90 million. By doing so, the exporter has avoided selling at the current spot rate of 1.0810, which would have resulted in proceeds of €10.81 million. While the knock-out put option has provided the exporter a gross notional profit of €90,000, subtracting the cost of €50,000 gives the exporter a net profit of €40,000.

(2) The U.S. dollar is trading exactly at the strike price of € 1.0900. In this case, it makes no difference if the exporter exercises the put option and sells at the strike price of Euro 1.0900, or sells in the spot market at € 1.0900. (In reality, however, the exercise of the put option may result in payment of a certain amount of commission). The loss incurred is the amount of premium paid, 50 pips or €50,000.

(3) The U.S. dollar is trading above the strike price of € 1.0900. In this case, the put option will expire unexercised and the exporter will sell the US$10 million in the spot market at the prevailing spot rate. The loss incurred in this case is the amount of premium paid, 50 pips or €50,000.

Binary Options

Binary Options are options that allow 'binary' decisions (yes / no) on spot forex pairs. For example, an investor can choose if EUR/USD will be 'up' or 'down' in the next 60 seconds. The expiry of binary options contracts is usually very small, and brokers will offer choices such as 1 minute, 15 minute, 30 minute, and 1 hour. Usually brokers will cap the investment amount of a binary options contract, because there is no 'market' for binary options – they are all OTC (Over the Counter) contracts. Because binary options is a completely opaque OTC contract, it has given the rise to many unregulated, unscrupulous companies offering binary options. Many will have professional looking websites and even include words like 'bank' in their name, providing the illusion of credibility. But they are just bucket shops, where it's nearly impossible to win against them. This is possible because in this opaque OTC market, the broker is on the other side of the contract. So if you win or lose, it's the decision of the broker. Playing binary options with these companies is a little like playing the game, guess how many fingers are behind my back.

Multicurrency debt swaps

Multi-currency debt swaps are OTC (Over the Counter) derivatives whereby 2 parties agree to 'swap' currencies against their debt. The major difference between Forex swaps and Forex debt swaps is the addition of the debt component. But practically, they are 2 separate contracts not related to each other, except that the initiating party is motivated to swap because they both worry about their debt payment obligations against fluctuating currencies. Because of the international lending market, it's possible for large corporations and governments to borrow in more than their own functional currency. So those who have good managers utilize such instruments to hedge their Forex risk, such as if they were borrowing in their local currency.

Currency debt swaps are so opaque and misunderstood, even the WSJ has it wrong[cv]:

And while we can't deny our almost preternatural understanding of international finance, we must admit that even we need some help from time to time.

For instance, we confess to being somewhat flummoxed by the role "currency swaps" seemed to be playing in the ongoing saga of Greece's wobbly financial condition. In today's Heard on the Street, the Journal's Richard Barley writes that Europe's official numbers crunching body has decided "to ask Greece for more details on currency swaps it may have used to defer debt repayments," a move Barley says "has reminded investors that all governments have huge long-term lurking liabilities not disclosed in their accounts."

The closest the Financial Times came to an explainer was this passage on Greece and the arranger of some of these transactions, Goldman Sachs: "It is hard to deny that the Goldman deal did create an optical illusion. It involved some €5bn of currency swaps at off-market rates and its effect was to let Greece borrow money without recording it as part of its public liabilities."

An anonymous user comment summarizes the simplicity of Forex vs. the mainstream understanding:

- Mr. Swap wrote :

The currency swaps are nothing but a series of FX forward contracts that convert principal and interest of debt in one currency into that of another currency. These are simple and widely used. They are NOT complex or nefarious in any way. Companies and governments routinely borrow in different capital markets to diversify their sources of funding and then swap the FX debt back to their functional currency. The combination of the FX debt plus the swap will be economically equivalent to the borrowing in their functional currency. So USD debt + USD to EUR currency swap = synthetic EUR debt. The news stories on this seem to have it wrong. They report that Goldman paid Greece cash and entered into off market swaps so that the FX rate was not at current market and then Greece would report a smaller EUR liability. This is incorrect. If Goldman paid Greece money, then the equivalent EUR debt would actually be at a higher value, not lower. **Strange how people are reporting on this story who seem to know what they are talking about but really have no clue. This isn't fair to Goldman at all.**

Thanks Mr. Swap! Forex debt swaps are extremely opaque and misunderstood, but fairly simple mathematically speaking. As far as derivatives go, they are a 9th grade level of complexity. By using vanilla Forex hedging tools such as forwards, options, futures, and other instruments; it's possible to create an FX synthetic scenario for virtually any circumstance.

Multi-currency debt swaps are usually customized instruments created by investment banks for specific situations, usually in between 2 parties. But if the 2 counterparties don't match, an Investment Bank (IB) may create the instrument and try to find a buyer. A Forex debt swap is the same as an FX Swap, but instead of a pure FX swap (when one currency is 'swapped' for another), debt is swapped. What makes it seemingly more complex is the valuation of the debt in 2 different currencies, but really it's not so different from a cash FX Swap. Often, debtors will take a significant haircut – even as much as 50% or even 90%, in order to find a buyer. This is common in developing countries where it's difficult to find a bond investor domestically. Foreign banks will buy the debt at pennies on the dollar, often converting the debt into equity of some sort. The Forex element makes such deals all the more attractive. In some rare cases, central banks will create special Forex prices for foreign banks, as an investment incentive. So FX Debt Swaps can be a very profitable business for banks – with very little risk (as the debt is usually secured by some significant collateral.)

In the most basic form – imagine that you have US Dollar (USD) debt in any form; a mortgage. You want to buy a house in Germany, but the house you want has a mortgage too. You could swap the USD mortgage for the EUR mortgage outright by using an Investment Bank. The spread for such a transaction would be high, but probably a lot less than the hassle of selling the house domestically, paying it off, and then refinancing in EUR when the house in Germany is finally purchased. Also you would still be subject to a high USD to EUR conversion fee, assuming you used a traditional bank. Although this is extremely rare on a retail level, businesses do this all the time, especially international companies in heavy industries, where for example the selling of a factory is complicated and costly.

8.5 The Penny Splitter Forex Strategy

"Splitting Pennies" as an educational metaphor, and practical learning tool for those who do not understand Forex, is best represented by an actual trading strategy. So all readers and owners of this book, are entitled to receive their free copy of "Penny Splitter" Forex robot. If you have not already done so, you can get your free copy at www.splittingpennies.com

Penny Splitter Instruction Manual

Description and use

"Penny Splitter" is an automated Forex algorithmic strategy, coded in MQL4 format, and compliant with the new build 600 directive. In order to trade the strategy, you will need a Meta Trader 4 or 5 terminal; to trade the strategy live, you must have an account opened with a broker that offers this software platform. All related software, information, support, and account opening links for SP (Splitting Pennies) owners and SFIs (Sophisticated Forex Investors) available at www.splittingpennies.com

The strategy 'splits' any currency pair into micro cents, using many small orders. Penny Splitter is a counter trend strategy that means if the Forex pair is going up, Penny Splitter is a seller. This can be counterintuitive for traders who learned to trade on stock, commodity, or bond markets. Because for example, when stocks trend, they can do so for years and even decades. This is not true in Forex – with a few rare exceptions.

Using default settings, the strategy uses 'negative leverage' meaning that on a 10,000 account, the initial trade can start at 1,000 units (or .01). The trade size increases as the pair moves, this is called 'legging in' to a trade. By this method of trade entry, it should not matter when Penny Splitter is loaded.

Expert Advisors Forex Robots are commonly converted to the MQL language for their ease of use, and because there are thousands of Meta Trader brokers in the world. Forex Robots that work in Meta Trader are called "Expert Advisors" and are represented by a creepy faceless character with a blue hat tilted to one side. In order to activate Penny Splitter, it must be first copied to the /experts folder of your trading terminal. Then to activate the strategy, choose the pair and timeframe you want to trade (such as EUR/USD 1 hour) and drag the Penny Splitter EA to the chart.

Then you can check your settings – the settings will determine how the strategy trades! Always double check the settings. Every action taken by Penny Splitter automatically is logged in the 'experts' tab, and all other trading related events are logged in the 'journal' tab. In case of errors or problems, this will be the first piece of information requested by a technician.

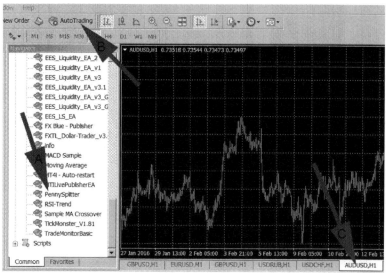

Once you've checked the settings and you're ready to see the fun start, press [Above Figure 6 A - Penny Splitter EA B – Auto Trading toggle on/off C – Currency pair and timeframe chart window] the Auto Trading button on the top of the screen, and Penny Splitter will immediately open 2 trades – buy and sell. Then it will continue to open more orders until account protection is reached, or the strategy is stopped. The entry logic of the strategy is described in the algorithm:

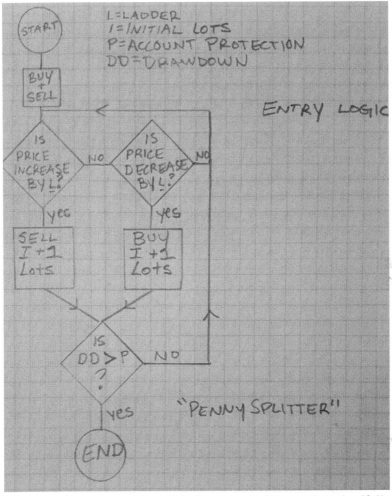

If the pair goes up by "L" then sell "IL + 1" Lots; if the pair goes down by "L" then buy "IL + 1" Lots. Each order, buy and sell, has the same simple TP (Take Profit) which is a static integer. In parallel runs Account Protection (AP) which acts as a per pair stop loss, calculated in percentage drawdown (loss). This is critical to understanding how the strategy works – Penny Splitter will run until the AP is reached. AP is set as a percentage of the account; so if AP = 5%, and the loss on the pair is 5% or greater, the strategy will close on that pair only. So, if Penny Splitter is loaded on 5 currency pairs, with an AP of 5 on each, there is a theoretical max loss of 25% of the account value. Although it seems 'negative' to discuss losses so much, if losses can be managed and limited, all that is left is profits.

Penny Splitter is not spread dependent, but the lower the cost of trading, the more money it will make.

Penny Splitter is designed as a framework, not a 'set and forget' style system that means by changing the parameters, it can become a completely different strategy.

Order sizing

Penny Splitter will open 2 orders (buy and sell) using the value in 'initial lots' parameter, and then increase size by counting in parallel with trade number. If the default initial lot size is 1, the size will be increased sequentially as 1,2,3,4,5,6,7,8 and so on. Changing the 'Multiplier' parameter will multiply each new order by the multiplier amount, sequentially. This can be very dangerous – so only change this if you really know what you are doing! For example, a multiplier of 2 would mean orders would be sized as 1,2,4,8,16,32,64...

Default Parameters

Trade Buy=true // If true strategy will place buy orders, default is setting BOTH buy and sell to true
Trade Sell=true // If true strategy will place sell orders, default is setting BOTH buy and sell to true

Magic Number=12358912 //Magic number should be different on each chart in order to avoid order confusion

Slippage=1 //Max slippage allowed in pips

Ladder=2 //Distance of grid level. New orders will be generated when the price goes up or down by this amount, in pips

Max Trade=9999 //Maximum total trades allowed to be open at any given time. This can be used to limit the total amount of trades that can be placed.

Take Profit=2 //Take profit of each order, usually the same value as Ladder

Stop Loss=1800 //Stop loss of each trade, should be placed 200 - 300 pips away from current price. Add a zero for 5 digit server.

Initial Lots=0.1 //Lot size for each order

Close Percent=25 //Account Protection level in percentage, will stop trading if this percent loss is reached

Timer= 99999 //Number in hours before system will close all orders. Set to 99999 for unlimited (then reset after 99999 hours)

Multiplier= 1.0 //Number to multiply each successive grid level by. Set to 2 for martingale, set to 1 for normal grid.

The most important parameters are the Ladder, Take Profit, and Close Percent (Account Protection). These 3 parameters define the behavior of the strategy such as amount of trades, amount of risk, and frequency of trades. Normally, the ladder and take profit are the same – but it's not required. The higher these 2 numbers, the less risky the strategy is and the less frequently it will trade. These parameters should be optimized per pair, for example the best value to use on EUR/USD may be 17, and the best on USD/JPY 12, and the best on GBP/USD 35. Because each pair has different trading behavior, different volatility, different spreads, and so on. Setting both default to a value greater than 30 can allow for a reasonable amount of trades, without huge risk.

THERE IS ALWAYS RISK IN FOREX TRADING – no matter how many stop losses, account protections, and other money management features we can add to any strategy, it doesn't eliminate the risk. Trading is all about managing risk! Risk in real terms, can be measured by size. If you don't want a big risk, trade small sizes relative to your account, and make use of account protection. For example, if you have a 50,000 account and load Penny Splitter with 2% account protection on a particular pair – your loss will be limited to $1,000. In rare cases, the loss could be more – for example if your internet or power goes out and the terminal is not able to execute trades.

Meta Trader handles all order management on the client terminal. That means if your computer running the terminal crashes, or your power goes out, trades will not be executed. For this reason, most traders use a dedicated server or VPS located near their broker. 90% of VPS providers utilize the same datacenters such as NY4, so that your computer is physically near your counterparty. In many cases, VPS providers' hookup physical fiber cables to Forex banks & brokers and offer an "on-net" service, similar to trading over a LAN (Local Area Network). Top tier services have 99.99% uptimes and even in situations such as recent Hurricane's which have threatened infrastructure, redundant backup systems were able to provide seamless uninterrupted service to customers. Almost more importantly, such a VPS setup puts you several MS (Millisecond) away from your counterparty. With most strategies, a few MS latency will not affect trading – but it sure doesn't help to have high latency to your counterparty. Also, during times when the market is very active, such as during NFP or major news announcement, even broker servers can become clogged with orders, and orders with lower pings may have an advantage when the market is moving quickly.

Because there are so many nuances to trading Forex Robots, one should either make a significant time investment, or select an established Forex manager who can advise through the process or via a managed account.

See the example of a test run using 25 as the Ladder and Take Profit, on the NZD/USD (New Zealand Dollar) from January until March 2016:

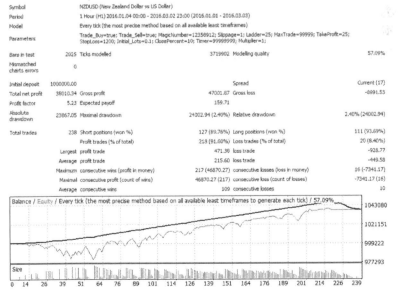

Running tests is a great way to see how certain parameters would do. It's important to have high quality tick data which is hard to come by these days, but any test will provide a general idea of a strategy's performance, even though it may be just a rough estimate. For optimization of parameters, it is sufficient to use data provided by the demo of the broker inside the terminal. For more professional development purposes, service providers sell testing data and other tools for a fee, which can be plugged into the MT4 system.

The strategy is a 'hedged grid' or 'grid inside of grid.' A grid strategy is one that buys and sells above and below the current price at certain levels, usually static levels called 'ladder.' Explicitly, running a pure grid will probably eventually blow up (trader lingo for 'lose') because the pair will trade out of the range. For example, EUR/CHF was 'pegged' into a range by the SNB (Swiss National Bank) for a long period of time, but then was allowed to 'breakout' of this range. So during this range, any grid would have done well – but would have been crushed during the breakout. Penny Splitter is not a pure grid, or martingale system – it does use a grid style methodology to trade entry. Successful grid strategies that work for many years, usually target a low profit target (such as 2% per month – yes that's low for Forex!) and do not use very much leverage. Also, they utilize highly optimized parameters, and a flexible or dynamic grid; such that the grid becomes really a framework, not a trading method. This approach works because while Forex can be volatile, Central Banks will prevent extreme volatility – for example we could not see the EUR/USD move 20% in one day.

Parameter basics

Changing of the settings can greatly change the behavior of the strategy. Actually – the strategy is the settings! And don't forget the most important setting – the trader. By choosing the pair, timeframe, and when the strategy begins, the trader also influences the results. This is one reason why this strategy given to 100 traders will produce 100 different results. Remember that the <u>parameters are per pair, and per time frame – this is referred to as an 'instance.'</u> By making use of the magic number, it's possible to use Penny Splitter in 2 different ways on the same pair – for example, EUR/USD scalper (short term) and EUR/USD long term. By using a unique Magic Number on each chart, it eliminates the possibility of order confusion. Meta Trader 4 allows for an infinite number of instances, although as you add many (such as more than 20 or 30) it can cause resource issues if you are using a normal Windows Desktop computer.

Stop Loss

There are several ways to limit Penny Splitter with parameters, other than the global stop loss "Account Protection." One is the "Stop Loss" which is a per trade stop loss. Typically, in a grid style environment a stop loss would ruin the goal of the strategy because the whole idea of such a strategy is to 'wait' until the market reverses. However, if the grid is set such that it generates very few trades, a stop loss can take out positions very far away from the market that are not likely to ever come into profit. So for example, by setting a stop loss of 400 or 600 pips, if the strategy was able to sustain such a move, it would begin to exit trades with 500+/- pip losses. Normally, this setting should be set to a number so high it will never get hit. It was included because there are circumstances where per trade stop losses make sense. Another use of this parameter is if the strategy is being used in 'buy only' or 'sell only' mode, not in grid mode.

Buy only or Sell only mode
If a trader has a fundamental view on a currency and needs an entry algorithm, this is a great way to use Penny Splitter to achieve a specific goal. For example, let's assume that a trader is bearish on GBP/USD for fundamental reasons related to the British economy. Currencies will not reflect economic fundamentals immediately, as real money flows are determined by a number of factors; many of which are haphazard. By setting **Trade Buy to 'false' and Trade Sell to 'true'** – Penny Splitter would look to sell GBP/USD at every ladder as defined by the 'ladder' parameter, and so on. No buy orders would be opened at all. In this manner, Penny Splitter is stripped of its intelligence and used as an execution only algorithm.

Timer
The timer will turn off the system, including the closing of all orders, after the number of hours displayed. For example if Timer is set to '5' the system will close all orders after 5 hours. The Timer is a great way to capture low volume, low volatility markets before a data announcement. For example, in the hours preceding NFP or a Fed announcement, markets become very quiet in anticipation of the number. For 10, sometimes 20 or more hours the market will move in a very small trading range. Penny Splitter can capture this profit and then turn itself off before the announcement. In this case, be very sure to check the

settings against the time of the announcement – and ensure that you consider the time zone. Timer is not connected to any time zone, it is just a number of hours. It works well in combination with a very low ladder and take profit, such as 2 – 6; because when the Forex market is quiet – it's VERY quiet. The other point to note is that during such times, ONLY a system such as this can profit. It's range trading, via robot.

Max Trade

This is another way to limit Penny Splitter from opening a huge amount of orders simply by limiting the amount of orders the EA can open per pair. Max Trade means that for each instance of Penny Splitter, the robot will not open more orders than this value. This can be a good limitation in case the market explodes (trader lingo for move large in one direction) but still doesn't violate the account protection.

Notes about Penny Splitter

It's a good idea from time to time close all orders and reset the system from zero. It's because after a period of weeks and months, although the market may generally range and Penny Splitter does well, it can slowly creep into a 'new' range. This can be done manually, or by use of the timer. Setting the timer to 800 would close Penny Splitter after about 1.5 months. Only trading days are counted (this should be the case with most such settings).

The lower the ladder/TP number, the higher the frequency of trades, and the higher the risk. The lower the ladder/TP number, the lower the risk and lower the profit. To use Penny Splitter as a low frequency countertrend strategy, set the ladder and TP to a very high level such as 50, 75, or even 100 – and load it on a basket of 10 or more pairs.

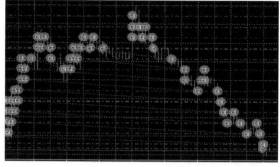

The best way to learn how to use it – trade it! Just be sure to use it extensively on a demo account before going live with real money. Included with the strategy are templates that have default parameters for specific sub strategies / iterations. Penny Splitter can really be used in a thousand different ways – in the most extreme way, to trade all the pairs all the time – every tick! If you have an idea about how Penny Splitter could be useful – run it through the tester! Due to the open framework design, test results for Penny Splitter are very accurate. That's because the parameters are few and logic is simple (it wouldn't matter so much if there is a few pips slippage, and other variables that may be different during a strategy test). The visual tester is a good way to 'visualize' how Penny Splitter would have traded.

Penny Splitter is a great teaching tool to understand how Forex really works more than other strategies – because Penny Splitter isn't a strategy per se, it's a doctrine and a framework. It's directionless (meaning – there is no indicator, and it doesn't matter if market goes up or down) and mathematically simple. At the same time, it's dynamic – by changing 'ladder' parameter, it can become a completely different strategy. For those who have never traded electronically before, a general education course available free on SP website and about the Meta Trader 4 platform is a necessary primer for using Penny Splitter. As you begin to use it on a demo, it will open up the real world of Forex from another part of the brain, based on practical example and real life operation. From this perspective, don't try to make money with it, try to understand how it works – and ideas will come to you as you watch it trade in different market conditions. Try loading it with a ladder of 2 and Take Profit of 2 when the market is quiet. Try it on all pairs with default settings and watch it behave. Test, test, test, and test again before going live!

Although Penny Splitter was designed for Forex, it could theoretically work on any market. However, its design is based on the fundamental view that Forex is a range bound countertrend market – generally. That means trading this on stocks, commodities, or other markets is not advisable. Also note that due to the fact that Penny Splitter is trading constantly, it can generate a high amount of commissions. If commissions are not built into the spread, beware of this when setting your ladder and take profit, to account for the per trade commission. Also note that the spread can be an issue on non-major pairs (exotics) such as USD/RUB, USD/MXN, and others. Due to trading restrictions, Penny Splitter may not work on all brokers. For more information, visit www.splittingpennies.com

9: Forex Future

Here we begin the real *open* book! From the date of publishing, this book nearly becomes irrelevant – because Forex changes so quickly, it can only be a footnote of financial history. Who knows how long the US Dollar will be the world reserve currency, and what digital currencies such as Bitcoin will challenge the role of traditional central bank backed currencies. Forex is full of black swan events. No one outside of the Nixon administration would have known that Nixon would just 'default' on US Forex obligations, creating a floating regime. No one outside of the SNB would have guessed, that the SNB would effectively destroy their currency at the whims of their US bosses. And recently, many would have agreed that the Chinese Yuan would replace the US Dollar as the new global reserve currency. But as China is on the brink of collapse, that doesn't look likely in the next 20 years at least. No one can see into the future, especially now with near zero latency execution at multiple regional FX ECNs. One thing is for sure, Forex will be at the center of a revolution in financial innovation based on new technologies that are waiting to be implemented.

The excitement is left to you – to speculate, imagine, develop, and shape the new global Forex community.

Some critical milestones to consider, for committee:

- The establishment of an international Forex 'exchange' such as a stock exchange.

- .FX a secure, private TLD reserved only for Forex trading, Forex banks, and Forex information.
- Opening up of Fed policy and books, as a matter of international example.
- Inclusion of Forex education in basic math & finance education programs for all children.
- Expansion of protocols such as FIX for the entire FX business, not only spot trading.
- US Banks consider offering Forex products, hedging tools, non-USD accounts.

Forex strategies will continue to play a critical role in the investment markets and in business. Because of 'globalization' and the internet, Forex is now inextricably tied into business and trading. In Forex, there is such a thing as a free lunch. That's because central banks print more new money to support the debt based financial system. By understanding and implementing a Forex doctrine, it provides a bird's eye view of the global economy, or 'super-macro' view. Forex is the super system that drives the global markets. It can be used both as an asset class per se, but more importantly a foundation for development of real business. Forex itself is an abstraction, an artificiality. It was invented by necessity, by politicians, not by economists or mathematicians. But nature found a balance and Forex is largely not volatile. Nature can be seen in Forex in Fibonacci numbers "The Magic Number." Technologies such as Block chain are revolutionizing the way trading is handled and accounted for. As one company TO (t0.com) says – "The Trade IS The Settlement.[cvi]" All of these new technologies combined with a fully electronic Forex system will create the new super paradigm of the global financial system. The reason the US Dollar became the world reserve currency it is now, was for only one reason – after WW2 it was the only alternative, and it worked. Just like foreigners trusted the Americans after WW2, a new generation of digital users will trust a secure, stable, encrypted digital financial system. As the system becomes more efficient, 'financial services' as a sector will become less relevant, and look more like a utility. The sector will be dominated by a small group of large, dominant players. Foreign exchange will eventually morph into 'financial exchange' as currencies become digital, and exchanged domestically. Markets and exchanges will be merged, as it will be possible to buy stocks in Euros and sell Wheat futures in Yen. Now that markets are fully electronic, this has become an exercise in enterprise I.T. management. Already, finance majors are being replaced by "Quants" with physics backgrounds. Algorithms are replacing traders, data centers are replacing trading floors.

It isn't possible to extrapolate this development by linear function – nor is it possible to predict what the Forex future will look like. We can only imagine, speculate, and develop!

Cybersecurity will play a big role, given the fully electronic nature of Forex. Recently, a group of Russian hackers traded another banks' funds in the USD/RUB market, significantly affecting the market price[cvii]. During a period that lasted about 14 minutes, the hackers traded about $400 Million USD worth of the contract. Normally this would be a drop in the big Forex bucket – but USD/RUB is very thinly traded. So the hackers were able to walk away with a hefty profit, leaving the bank to deal with an abnormal USD/RUB position. Why not, state sponsored hackers could break into the Fed and print Quadrillions of US Dollars and flood the market? Not a likely scenario, but something to consider in light of this bank security breach. The future of Forex will need security, encryption, and robust IT systems to manage it.

But for any future Forex system there is an educational Paradox. Imagine the ideal Forex system is created, it would require all who use it become knowledgeable about it – but we don't understand our current system! For this perfect monetary system, we should make educational courses and integrate them in our knowledgebase, business, and educational programs. But we aren't doing that with the existing Forex system. Now that we are near the end of this book, hopefully readers have a grasp of what "Forex" really is. But how many people will read this book? Probably not millions, so still only a drop in the bucket. Like with any new paradigm, knowledge and education is the only real driver. So in some way, we have currently the ideal Forex system. It's equivalent to saying that the population always gets the politicians it deserves.

9.1 Future Currencies
Although Fiat central bank issued currencies dominate the global landscape, in the past 10 years many small local currencies have been tested and used. Some are still in use today. They take various forms and shapes, but all have the same characteristics of money: a medium of exchange.

Some like Bitcoin are completely digital, others involve a 'barter' element in a local community. Even the IRS has rules about Virtual Currencies[cviii]:

WASHINGTON — The Internal Revenue Service today issued a notice providing answers to frequently asked questions (FAQs) on virtual currency, such as bitcoin. These FAQs provide basic information on the U.S. federal tax implications of transactions in, or transactions that use, virtual currency.

In some environments, virtual currency operates like "real" currency -- i.e., the coin and paper money of the United States or of any other country that is designated as legal tender, circulates, and is customarily used and accepted as a medium of exchange in the country of issuance -- but it does not have legal tender status in any jurisdiction.

The notice provides that virtual currency is treated as property for U.S. federal tax purposes. General tax principles that apply to property transactions apply to transactions using virtual currency. Among other things, this means that:

- *Wages paid to employees using virtual currency are taxable to the employee, must be reported by an employer on a Form W-2, and are subject to federal income tax withholding and payroll taxes.*
- *Payments using virtual currency made to independent contractors and other service providers are taxable and self-employment tax rules generally apply. Normally, payers must issue Form 1099.*
- *The character of gain or loss from the sale or exchange of virtual currency depends on*

whether the virtual currency is a capital asset in the hands of the taxpayer.

- *A payment made using virtual currency is subject to information reporting to the same extent as any other payment made in property.*

Further details, including a set of 16 questions and answers, are in Notice 2014-21, posted today on IRS.gov.

As of this writing, there are 2,500 local currencies operating throughout the world[cix]. While they remain 'local' and still are in no position to compete as a dominant financial, monetary alternative; their presence and widespread use should not be underestimated, when considering the Forex future. For example, Bitcoin was seen only several years ago as something for hackers and geeks. Suddenly, the New York State Department of Financial Services offers Bit License, so that merchants can accept payments in Bitcoin[cx]. It's now possible to pay for a restaurant meal, at select establishments, using Bitcoin. All of this transformation has happened so quickly. Technology platforms, widespread use of broadband internet, and a desire to use secure encrypted financial systems, have provided the right opportunity for this rapid development. A generation of users who grew up online, and then with mobile phones, adapted to this financial technology easily. But the key difference that made Bitcoin useful, were the Bitcoin exchanges.

Ultimately, users needed to transfer their Bitcoin into US Dollars to feel more comfortable using the digital currency. Digital currencies, local currencies, and new state backed currencies will ultimately make the Forex markets of the future more dynamic.

The state of South Carolina created a subcommittee to determine if the state should issue its own currency as an alternative to the Federal Reserve System, in the event of financial collapse, hyperinflation, or severe market disruption [cxi]. Other states have supported similar measures, although until now none have passed. But it would not be so unusual, especially since many of these states used to have their own state backed currencies, such as the South Carolina Pound[cxii].

9.11 One World Currency

The idea of a single currency used in the entire world has been circulated both in academic circles and by conspiracy theorists on the internet alike. But is a one world currency really practical? Only if we would also have a one world government, which is not a likely scenario. It would mean the subjugation of all countries to one central bank, whether it be the BIS (Bank of International Settlements) or some newly formed Super-Central Bank. A country is a currency, not only in terms of economic value, but in terms of sovereignty. EU members have given up this right to participate in the European Union and the Euro. While there has not been a country that has decided to leave the Euro yet, a "Grexit" scenario has been on the possibility horizon for some time[cxiii]:

The **Greek withdrawal from the eurozone** is the potential <u>exit</u> of <u>Greece</u> from the <u>eurozone</u> <u>monetary union</u>, primarily for the country or <u>its government</u> to deal with <u>its public debt</u>. The controversial and much discussed possible exit is often referred to in financial circles as "**Grexit**", a <u>portmanteau</u> combining the words "Greek exit". Proponents of the proposal argue that leaving the <u>euro</u> and reintroducing the <u>drachma</u> would dramatically boost exports and tourism and encourage the local economy while discouraging expensive imports. Opponents argue that the proposal would impose excessive hardship on the Greek people, cause civil unrest, destabilize and harm the reputation of the eurozone, and could cause Greece to align more with non-EU states.

Greece is an example of the far left of the spectrum in the debate, to secede or not from the Union. The European Union is very similar to the United States from a currency perspective (states such as South Carolina used to be their own countries, with their own currencies). The European Union has provided the world with an excellent use case model of how countries can give up their sovereignty for a Supercurrency, with all its benefits and problems. We don't need to analyze sociology or macroeconomics in too much detail, to realize that a one world currency is impractical. Considering the most extreme examples, imagine Russia, China, and India giving up their sovereignty to a one world government, connected somehow to a one world central bank. If that's not a challenging enough example to draw the conclusion, imagine the hundreds of countries that do actually maintain their own currencies, such as the Swiss Franc, and hundreds of others. There are 180 currencies currently in use in the world[cxiv]. From one perspective, the US Dollar is already a de facto one world currency. Depending on how you count, it's used as a peg for about 20 currencies. It's used as a reserve currency for virtually every currency on the planet, even the Russian Ruble. So if there is to be a 'one world currency' it's probably going to be the US Dollar, even if only metaphorically speaking. We can even say about it now – the US Dollar is a one world currency.

Proposals for future currencies have been interesting. Hugo Chavez proposed a "Petro Currency" to be backed by Oil producing nations[cxv]:

DOHA, Qatar (AP) — Venezuelan President Hugo Chavez sought Arab support Tuesday for his idea of a new oil-backed currency to challenge the U.S. dollar at a twin-region summit whose agenda focuses on trade issue but also touches on Arab worries about rival Iran's growing influence in Latin America. It's highly unlikely Chavez will gain any serious momentum for his "petro-currency" proposals from key oil-producing members of the Arab League such as Saudi Arabia and Gulf states, which have close ties to Washington.

Such proposed currencies[cxvi] serve as good examples to show that while a new currency system may be more efficient or preferable than the current system, without political support they are not likely to succeed. But it is again a Forex paradox, because the only way we can have political support for a system is through education via marketing campaigns. At the end of the day, bankers rule the world, because they can print money and buy as many politicians as they need. It comes down to what serves their purpose. When evaluating what may be in store for the Forex future, bear in mind the power driven realities of how our world works. But sometimes, the mother of invention is necessity. Many macro analysts are convinced that the next 20 years will be filled with financial calamity, volatility, and a revolution of the global financial system. One such banker is Bernard Lietaer, a relatively unknown banker who literally had the only model of Forex after the Nixon Shock:

Bernard Lietaer, the author of <u>The Future of Money: Beyond Greed and Scarcity</u> *and* <u>New Money for a New World</u>*, has been active in the realm of* <u>money systems</u> *for close to 40 years in a wide variety of functions. With the publication of his post-graduate thesis at MIT in 1971· (which included a description of "floating exchanges") and the* <u>Nixon Shock</u> *of that same year which eradicated the* <u>Bretton Woods system</u> *by unhinging the US dollar value from its gold standard and inaugurated the new era of universal floating exchanges (previous to that time the only "floating exchanges" involved some exotic currencies in Latin America), the fledgling management consultant suddenly found himself to be at the center of the financial world's attention. The techniques that he had developed for those marginal Latin American currencies were overnight the only systematic research which could be used to deal with all of the major currencies of the world. A major US bank negotiated exclusive rights to his approach which required that he begin another career.[2] While at the Central Bank in Belgium (<u>National Bank of Belgium</u>) he* implemented the convergence mechanism (ECU) to the single European currency system. During that period, he also served as President of Belgium's Electronic Payment System. His consultant experience in monetary aspects on four continents ranges from multinational corporations to developing countries.

Lietaer has argued that the world's national currencies are inadequate for the world's business needs, citing how 87 countries have experienced major currency crashes over a 20-year period, and arguing for complementary currencies as a way to protect against these problems. His most interesting proposal for a world currency protected from inflation, is the "Terra" a currency based on a basket of the world's 9-12 most important commodities, determined by their importance in worldwide trade. Originally published in France in the publication "Le Fédériste" on 1 January 1933, the idea has a solid mathematical foundation. But the modern global power structure has so many incentives to maintain the current system, so many conflicts, and so many barriers to destruction, it seems it will take a real financial meltdown to effect any change. Modern debt based fiat money is literally sucking real value from the real economy like a big black hole. The reason the economy gets worse and worse each year, in all countries, is because of the American Forex System. One important thing to understand about a debt based financial system where money printing is unchecked, the Elite bankers who control the system do not want to make money – because they can easily print as much as they want for themselves. They want to make other people poor, and suck the real value from the real economy, such as working people, factories, farmers, and so on. Of course they are not aware of this, your friendly neighborhood banker even provides discounts on loans to the indigent, minorities, and other causes useful on the surface. The system is just designed like this. The US Dollar is a big game of hot potato – investors making 20% and even 50% a year in their portfolios, after taxes, are barely breaking even. Inflation is skyrocketing, and bankruptcy is built into the system, because it's impossible that ALL businesses pay back their loans plus interest.

But we will always have the best capital – that which is between our ears.

Because the only real currency is intelligence.

10: Addendum 1: Market Updates

In Forex, a day seems like a week. Well, it's been 2 long months since the original publication of Splitting Pennies, and already it's become an Amazon bestseller. Practically, it's not possible to update the book on a monthly basis, with all the changes in Forex that are happening in real-time. But that's why we have blogs. We've included in this exclusive addendum, 3 important articles from our blog.

5/18/2016

10.1 Mind Control as a method to support the US Dollar

There is a paradox of capitalism, we've reached a point where those at the top, have an unlimited budget to maintain the status quo, increase their wealth, and develop an ever increasing sophisticated toolbox to manage empire and maintain their dominance. As we explain in Splitting Pennies - this is nowhere more obvious than Forex. The last 100 years we've seen capitalism evolve brightly. Industries that shouldn't be industries, now employ millions of workers. Paradigm shift, revolution, can now be artificially created by means of automated computer algorithm. The political process, has been hacked by this technology. And it's all controlled by a central banking Elite - it's all controlled by THEY (Them). At the top of the pyramid of society, groups such as the CIA, MI6, KGB, Mossad, and others - are responsible for maintaining safety and security, that is, from change. They cull the herd when necessary, whether it be a revolution in Libya, or bringing down the twin towers. But these are all physical ops, their most important missions are the ones least talked about - that is, PsyOps, and most significantly, PsyOps that support the financial system. I believe that if ZH readers can understand this matrix, it will help make better more objective investing decisions. Because although the market is a free entropic environment, it is controlled by humans, by institutions, and well - it's only free when it's allowed to be free. These PsyOps are what make such a state of hypocrisy possible - otherwise, people would 'wake up' and realize that we are programmed with oxi moron hypocrisy. "We had to bomb the village to save it." The tools they use to implement mind control are very simple and have been around for 50 years - the most successful one is Television (TV). According to testimony by CIA analyst who was involved in domestic PsyOps, he said when asked how the average person can avoid such programming, "Unplug your TV." In case you aren't aware of modern mind control techniques, checkout this well compiled article by Activist Post about 10 methods commonly used.

The connection between the global social control paradigm and the US Dollar runs deep. In support of the US Dollar, it's important that people are blindly hypnotized into submission by using US Dollars. This is more important than any Fed operations to prop the markets. Because ultimately, the only real threat to the US Dollar is if people start THINKING. At the end of the day, the US Dollar, like any fiat currency, provides a basic accounting service for economic activity. Never before in history has a single currency enjoyed such widespread global use. And the marketing and propaganda campaigns in support of the USD support it more than the Petro Dollar system, more than CIA operations in Switzerland, and more than any financial algorithm employed by groups such as the Plunge Protection Team (PPT). Understanding something, isn't criticizing - maybe it's a good thing, maybe not - it's not for the teacher to make any conclusive opinion. It is however something that all investors should be aware of, especially those who are subject to daily Neuro Linguistic Programming (NLP) in support of this financial system. Why is Hollywood so successful? Because they make magic - they make the artificial, seem real... if only for a few moments, it is enough to rewire your brain, already filled with advertising, chemicals in the food, air, and water, and various radio and radiation pumped into populated areas. The Fed, controlled by a similar group of people like Hollywood is, also makes magic. They make people believe in this paper they print numbers on called "Federal Reserve Notes" - even though it's backed by nothing. US Dollars are only backed by BELIEF and FAITH in them - which is why Mind Control - or in more plain language, aggressive advertising; is necessary to support the US Dollar.

Maybe watching some of these lunatics that have coined phrases such as "King Dollar" are enough for the average busy businessman to be lulled into a sense of semi-consciousness, where rational, objective thought is impossible. Buy buy buy.. drill drill drill.. Investors are whipped into a bullish frenzy easily with such programming. They meet the first criteria - they are open to it. Admitting you have a problem, is step number one. The mind is like a parachute, you must open to use. Not only that, they actually want to hear what TV personalities want to say, to help them make investing decisions! I remember when I learned Bill OReilly wrote a book - I was shocked. I didn't think that someone with his mental disability could even read - let alone write! (Still, I'm not sure he actually wrote any book, probably he hired someone to do it.) Anyway, this guy is a great example of someone who fits the role needed to be played perfectly - slightly mentally retarded, aggressive abrasive personality, with a lot of opinions about meaningless issues that will guarantee that it is impossible to receive any valuable information by watching such a program.

So how does this all work? Clearly, the Elite have decided that financial services - it's not for the people. People should work hard, obey, consume, watch sports, and watch TV, and eat, and drink.. So they embed advertising in subtle ways, when discussing financial issues. For example, during the 911 commission reports and investigation, there's no mention of the post 911 US Dollar, or transactions that took place short USD just before 911. There's a little talk about PUT options on UAL but they've tried confusing the issue by releasing Snopes reports that it's a myth, even though you can see what really happened here:

FTW, October 9, 2001 - Although uniformly ignored by the mainstream U.S. media, there is abundant and clear evidence that a number of transactions in financial markets indicated specific (criminal) foreknowledge of the September 11 attacks on the World Trade Center and the Pentagon. In the case of at least one of these trades -- which has left a $2.5 million prize unclaimed -- the firm used to place the "put *options" on United Airlines stock was, until 1998, managed by the man who is now in the number three Executive Director position at the Central Intelligence Agency. Until 1997 A.B. "Buzzy" Krongard had been Chairman of the investment bank A.B. Brown. A.B. Brown was acquired by Banker's Trust in 1997. Krongard then became, as part of the merger, Vice Chairman of Banker's Trust-AB Brown, one of 20 major U.S. banks named by Senator Carl Levin this year as being connected to money laundering. Krongard's last position at Banker's Trust (BT) was to oversee "private client relations". In this capacity he had direct hands-on relations with some of the wealthiest people in the world in a kind of specialized banking operation that has been identified by the U.S. Senate and other investigators as being closely connected to the laundering of drug money.*

Krongard (re?) joined the CIA in 1998 as counsel to CIA Director George Tenet. He was promoted to CIA Executive Director by President Bush in March of this year. BT was acquired by Deutsche Bank in 1999. The combined firm is the single largest bank in Europe. And, as we shall see, Deutsche Bank played several key roles in events connected to the September 11 attacks.

No mention of Forex - no USD short. No reports about the missing Gold from the Fed depository, which was at Ground Zero. This type of subtle manipulation goes on today. It's not what they say, it's what they don't say. As long as the American population is fat, happy, and stupid - they will be happy to use US Dollars, which continually decline in value. Alternatives such as community currencies, gold, Bitcoin, and others - which are readily available for use - should be avoided at all costs. Most Americans aren't even aware that other currencies exist. As we explain in our book Splitting Pennies - this brainwashing of the domestic population is critical to the global advertising campaign that supports the US Dollar. The USD is the one world currency. The Euro, backed by USD and run by CIA agent "Super Mario" - is simply the other side of the same coin.

The goal of this programming is simple - don't question the US Dollar. It's not about convincing people to buy USD in a Forex account. In fact, they're betting that by not questioning the value of the USD or questioning the USD as an accounting functional currency, people aren't going to want to trade Forex, where they can potentially hedge themselves from Forex exposure, or even make a fortune on Forex like Stan did. What's the point of this article? Turn off your TV, or just obey.

They are investing billions to control your mind. All they want is your time. Just a few moments of your time. It's all they need. Who cares, whatever, never mind.

10.2 The Forex Rigging Irony

While Forex banks, traders, and other institutions are being blamed for market rigging, the Swiss National Bank can publish reports about its own market rigging, but instead of being a scandal, it's economic data. That's because the vast majority don't understand how the Forex markets work. It's not insulting - it's a fact. Currently there are hundreds of pending litigation cases against a plethora of Forex banks, traders, and other institutions - but none against a central bank. Of course it would be ridiculous to sue a central bank for market rigging -

because it's in their mandate to manipulate the market. Of course they don't call it manipulation, they call it 'market operations' and the Fed, sometimes known as 'market intervention' or 'stabilization efforts.' Anyhow, it seems strange that on the one hand, central banks manipulate their own currency via 'market operations' which mostly are done through commercial Forex banks, but it is the Forex banks that receive this printed money that are sued, not the central banks.

But look from the CB perspective - what's the point of printing money if you can't use it to intervene in the market and prop your own currency?

From Fortress Capital (source: Bloomberg)[cxvii]:

The Swiss National Bank will probably stay on hold at its monetary policy meeting on March 17 as banks in the country are already facing pressure from negative interest rates, economists and strategists say in notes to clients. The fact that the euro remained broadly stable against Swiss franc after the European Central Bank meeting lessens pressure on the SNB to act this week. SNB may intervene in the forex market to stem the franc's appreciation.

The question in everyone's mind now - do these central banks really know what they are doing? I mean, is there a coordinated international policy? A conspiracy? A conspiracy would imply intelligence.

One perspective is to look at Forex markets from the perspective of those in power, the UHNWI, or 'them'

- 'they' or 'The Elite.' They have all the money they can possibly have - with this money they buy power, such as politicians, countries, people, etc. They can't buy anything more. So the only thing left is to ensure the status quo - or ensure as much as possible they maintain their position. One way to do this which is more subtle, is to destroy the money supply. By making currency worthless, or worth - less, any potential competition will be either wiped out or marginalized. Would-be billionaires and up and coming entrepreneurs who are out there in the 'real world' making business, are contained. It also affords them other opportunities, such as providing this fresh QE money to the private banks they actually own, allowing them to invest in HFT and other stat arb style investment strategies with virtually no risk, allowing them to grow their own portfolios at a level which is practically speaking, exponentially greater than the average investor. And if their investments fail, they can always bail themselves out - or as the trend is, tax savers and bail themselves in.

Remember, our financial system is created by rules that are constantly changing. Just as Central Bank are created they are destroyed. Russia being one of the newest Central Bank in the game; about 30 years old:

The Central Bank of the Russian Federation (Bank of Russia) was established July 13, 1990 as a result of the transformation of the Russian Republican Bank of the State Bank of the USSR. It was accountable to the Supreme Soviet of the RSFSR. On December 2, 1990 the Supreme Soviet of the RSFSR passed the Law on the Central Bank of the Russian Federation (Bank of

Russia), according to which the Bank of Russia has become a legal entity, the main bank of the RSFSR and was accountable to the Supreme Soviet of the RSFSR. In June 1991, the charter was adopted by the Bank of Russia. On December 20, 1991 the State Bank of the USSR was abolished and all its assets, liabilities and property in the RSFSR were transferred to the Central Bank of the Russian Federation (Bank of Russia), which was then renamed to the Central Bank of the Russian Federation (Bank of Russia). Since 1992, the Bank of Russia began to buy and sell foreign currency on the foreign exchange market created by it, establish and publish the official exchange rates of foreign currencies against the ruble.

If Russia can establish a new Central Bank, why can't the United States of America, Australia, Canada, or Germany? How close are we to a hyperinflationary trap, as happened during the 19th century?

Wildcat banking refers to the practices of banks chartered under state law during the periods of non-federally regulated state banking between 1816 and 1863 in the United States, also known as the Free Banking Era. This era, commonly described as an example of free banking, was not a period of true free banking, as banks were free of only federal regulation; banking was regulated by the states. The actual regulation of banking during this period varied from state to state.

According to some sources, the term came from a bank in Michigan that issued private paper currency with the image of a wildcat. After the bank failed, poorly backed bank notes became known as wildcat currency, and the banks that issued them as wildcat banks. However, according to others, wildcat meant a rash speculator as early as 1812, and by 1838 had been extended to any risky business venture. A common conception of the wildcat bank in Westerns and like stories was of a bank that left its safe somewhat ajar for depositors to see, in which the banker would display a barrel full of nails, grain or flour with a thin sprinkling of cash on top, thus fooling depositors into thinking it was a successful bank. The traditional view of wildcat banks describes them as distributing nearly worthless currency backed by questionable security (such as mortgages and bonds). These actions ended when note circulation by state banks was stopped after the passage of the National Bank Act of 1863. Mark Twain, in his autobiography, refers to the use of such currency in 1853, 'The firm paid my wages in wildcat money at its face value".

Certainly, our current system is better that which was used during the "Free Banking Era" because the fiat money today is NOT "worthless currency" - but Central Banks such as the SNB (Swiss National Bank) certainly are trying hard to make it such!

Forex isn't just a money market, it's the underpinning of all other markets (i.e. you sell your stocks for US Dollars).

10.3 America's Big Red Forex Button - MOST IMPORTANT FOREX FACT

We have written extensively on the topic of Forex and published an in-depth book about key points "Splitting Pennies - Understanding Forex" - and in the process we've learned **what investors don't know about Forex** and how it fuels market fears. So now we'd like to elaborate on the **MOST IMPORTANT FACT INVESTORS NEED TO KNOW ABOUT FOREX, and to a lesser extent the markets in general.**

America has in its possession **A BIG RED FOREX BUTTON** that can shut down US Dollar connected payment systems with one press. This button can halt stock markets, futures exchanges, money markets, all with one simple push. Probably, it looks something like this: **STOP**

This button will probably never be used, it was developed in case of financial emergency. But it's there - and the fact that it exists, makes a few bank managers and government workers sleep well at night. Such systems are developed 'just in case' - just like the missile defense system, a complete waste of taxpayer dollars, built to ensure that if nuclear missiles are launched on America, America can save 10% of cities and wipe out the majority of the attacker based on the neo-con 'mutually assured destruction' MAD policy. This button serves the same purpose, although financial. Pressing this button would bring all economic activity in economies that utilize the US Dollar to a complete standstill.

Lazy government workers

To understand why and how this button was built, we must first understand a little about how the US Government works. The US Government is the largest employer of any kind in the world. We need to understand the differences between private employment, and government employment (because this big red button was built by government workers in collaboration with private workers). Private employment operates on a simple market based approach - good workers are rewarded usually with higher pay, more job security, and more benefits. If a worker for a private company makes his company a fortune, he'll be rewarded with a big bonus, big desk with accompanying window, and an office plant, maybe a fern. If the worker in a private company is a bad worker, lazy, incompetent, or just difficult - he will be fired. Government is the opposite. There's a mantra in government work - what do you do with a problem employee? Promote them! Because then they are out of your hair, and if you fire them, well you may end up in front of a senate hearing explaining why, or you may end up being sued, or you may end up with a number of special interest groups heckling you about the rights of people with Narcolepsy.

The government approaches work in an entirely different way than in private enterprise. Healthcare.gov - the world's first billion dollar website, is another great example. Now imagine the task the Department of Defense is given; protect America from external threats. Their first step, to identify threats. In the military, this is done by agencies such as the CIA and the

NRO. Actually if the CIA operated according to its public mission, it would be an analyst agency not much different than those seen on Wall St. - providing information to their DOD bosses who act on it. Since 911, the potential for financial terrorism has been considered a national security issue. It's in the laws, it's in the regulations, and it's serious. What if the Saudis flood the market with US Dollars? What if the Chinese dump treasuries crashing the US Dollar? What if hackers take control of the NYSE and flood the market with sell orders, causing a crash? These are all extremely improbably events, so rare there is a higher chance of a giant meteor striking Manhattan this year. The probability is so low it's difficult to calculate. But just like the false threat of Russian's launching nukes, billions of dollars have been spent building a Big Red Button to press in case it happens.

It's because government workers have one thing in mind; protect themselves. Avoid a potential disaster. The last thing any government worker wants is to be in charge of security on a day like 911, even if the threat is financial. Although the debate rages about TARP and government actions during the weekend of the Bear Stearns collapse - the financial system was saved. They pressed the button. But this wasn't the Forex button.

Although the Federal Reserve is a private bank, the US Dollar exists because of the US Government. Like with many government projects, they outsource. More than 60% of CIA operations are currently outsourced. It's good business - America has always been like that. The only role the US

Government plays in the US Dollar, is providing regulations & oversight with the OCC (Office of the Comptroller of the Currency), and printing physical currency with the US Mint. But the US Mint is just a printing service, if you look on US bills you'll see "Federal Reserve Note."

The Big Red Forex Button

We've known for a long time about the infamous "Plunge Protection Team" designed to prop stock markets in the event of a 1987 style crash. They even have entities in the Caymans funded by the Fed ready and waiting - they'll start with buying futures on the S&P, then options, then if that fails, they'll just go into the market directly. Anyway, technically speaking, DTCC owns 99% of US securities being the only custodian for investors. Why should it be surprising that the Fed operates a Cayman based hedge fund specifically designed to prop the markets in the event of a crash?

And you know it's really ironic, it's PEAK HYPOCRISY - on the one hand, these right wing flag waving jingoists love the idea that we have a system in place to prevent a market crash by 100%, but on the other hand, they love to talk about how America has 'freedom' and 'free markets' and markets are not manipulated! Well we can't have our protection and free markets together. But probably, stock investors would agree, in the event of a big market crash it's probably best to have such systems in place, like we do for the military, and other critical infrastructure.

Does the PPT intervene in the markets on a daily, or regular basis? That's another question, probably, they do.. but we can say for sure they are there to soften the blow of a deep fall. Maybe they've done it more than once in the last 10 years, which is why the market is continually at nose bleed levels even though the real economy is in the toilet.

The Big Red Forex Button is simpler than the PPT, and similar organizations. That's because ALL US DOLLARS IN THE WORLD are created and processed by the Federal Reserve Bank! Except if you withdraw and deal with physical cash, the Fed has electronic tags and knows where each US Dollar in the world is. That's just how the system is setup, by design, by coincidence, it's just like that. The reason for the war on cash, it's really the only part of the US Dollar system that isn't 100% completely controlled and manipulated. But at the end of the day, with less than $1 Trillion in physical US Dollars in the world, it's not really significant. The Fed processes wire payments, ACH payments, clears checks, and provides US Dollars to central banks in the form of swaps. The Fed can press the Big Red Forex Button and halt all US Dollar transactions - period. So with a halt on all US Dollar transactions, how would China destroy the value of the US Dollar, as some have proposed? How would US Dollar debt holders repay their debt, without access to US Dollars? Everyone would default? The financial system would implode? No, they would just wait, for a Fed action. The Fed controls 100% of US Dollar transactions, globally. There's nowhere on this small planet Earth to 'hide' US Dollars.

The US Treasury has a similar tool, the US Treasury has a big red t-bill button. They can immediately recall or issue trillions of US debt in one click. As far as the external threat supposedly posed by foreign holders of US debt, if this really was a threat, the treasury can call their friends at the Fed, and in one click - the Fed can pay off all US debt. The Fed would be happy to do so, thus gaining free interest from US taxpayers (which is a HUGE percent of the Federal Budget) and it wouldn't cost the Fed anything to create the $100 Trillion or whatever necessary to do it.

Practically, there is no competition for America, and there will not likely be any in the foreseeable future. Just imagine if 10% of US Dollar assets were sold, and transferred to another currency, or another system. What would that currency be? It is a real problem. In order to entertain real scenarios of a 'US Dollar Collapse' we would need to see an alternative system, one which operates globally and completely without the US Dollar and it's institutions, such as the BIS, IMF, the Fed, ECB, SWIFT, such as Bitcoin.

But just to keep the size of the US Dollar in perspective, let's look at a real alternative - the New Zealand Dollar. Anyone with a Forex account can trade NZD/USD (when you trade a Forex pair, you're really betting on a rate change, not sending money to New Zealand, so trading Forex is a derivative). <u>The GDP of New Zealand is about $185 Billion.</u> There simply aren't enough investment options in New Zealand NZD based assets to facilitate any significant move into NZD from USD. In fact, NZD has been inflated by US and Chinese interests in the last 10 years, to the point that their GDP has nearly quadrupled since 2000.

Also remember that most currencies are backed by the US Dollar, so the only 'real' alternative to the US Dollar is not other currencies, but alternative systems such as Bitcoin.

One last correction about China - recently China has implemented a Gold fix denominated in Yuan. <u>Also Hungary has issued $154 Million in Yuan bonds.</u> These are both wonderful baby steps toward realizing the final goal of being a modern, dynamic, free market based economy. The Yuan IS NOT BACKED BY GOLD. China implemented a YUAN BASED GOLD MARKET, copied and pasted from the Rothschild-London dominated system for the last hundreds of years. The Gold price is set in Yuan, as it used to be in Great British Pounds. Separately, China is hoarding physical gold. These 3 facts do not mean that the Yuan is backed by Gold. Capital Controls are in place, the Yuan is manipulated by the central bank. It's not possible to do business with China via the Yuan like it is with G8 countries. Americans can visit and do business in hundreds of countries with ease, China is not one of them. China employs internet police, who will literally arrest you potentially for life if you are found violating their firewall policies. This is not a country which will soon compete with America, England, Switzerland, and the rest of the G8. India, possibly another story, but they have no plans to improve their Forex system or to be a global reserve currency.

Conclusion

The Federal Reserve controls all US Dollars created and transacted in the world, in collaboration with the US Government. The value of the US Dollar will fluctuate as interest rates change, and real money flows around the world affect supply and demand of the USD, but within a trading range. Forex markets are 100% controlled. At any point, Central Banks can intervene in Forex markets. We've never seen a collaborated intervention, but that's a possibility too. Because they all rely on each other, it's in their interest to see boring, non-volatile markets. They are all part of the same system, which is supported by America and the US Dollar.

If the Fiat central bank system would be to collapse, there would have to be an alternative system for the world's business to transition to. Currently, there is no alternative system in place. Many alternative systems are in the works, but they are decades from being complete. But in the meantime, there's a number of ways to profit in the Forex market, or protect yourself from market risks.

Appendix 1: Glossary

Common terms & abbreviations

USD - United States Dollars (USD)
IRS – The Internal Revenue Service
CEO – Chief Executive Officer
NSA – National Security Agency
NFA – National Futures Association
CFTC – Commodity Futures Trading Commission
FX – Forex, or Foreign Exchange
NFP- Non-Farm Payrolls
CIA – Central Intelligence Agency
EU – European Union
FIX – Financial Information Exchange
"The Fix" – WM/Reuters rates used for Forex
calculations, at a certain time such as 4PM London
FED – The Federal Reserve Bank
CHF – The Swiss Franc
Cable – The Great British Pound, named after the
undersea cable that connected New York to London
Yours – Sold – 'to you'
Mine – Bought – 'for me'
Piker – Someone who gambles in an unreasonable
way, such as by placing small bets in hope of a big
return, and then complains if it doesn't happen.
EA – Expert Advisor from the Meta Trader 4/5 platform,
i.e. "Robot"
"The Roll" – Rollover time, usually 5pm EST in New
York, when swaps are calculated and daily positions
calculated. Some banks & brokers will close for 15
minutes during this time.
POA or LPOA – Limited Power of Attorney, giving a
trader the right to trade your account.

Platform – The software used to access the market, through your bank / broker.

Dealing Desk – Software 'backend' used by Forex banks / brokers to trade against clients – literally. The dealer chooses what client order

Algo Trading – Algorithms, or software robots, that trade according to the instructions of the programmer.

Latency Arbitrage – Strategies that capture price differences based on network speed advantages, usually in different parts of the world.

Pip – Smallest unit of Forex movement as a standard, 1/10,000th of a position in a pair, i.e. EUR/USD is 1.2154 – the '4' is one pip

Appendix 2: References

References

Berlinski, D. (2001). *The Advent of the Algorithm.* Houghton Mifflin Harcourt.

Bianco, A. (2006). *The Bully of Bentonville.* Crown Publishing Group.

Fleming, V. (Director). (1939). *Gone with the Wind* [Motion Picture].

Friedman, T. (2005). *The World is Flat.* Farrar, Straus and Giroux.

Millman, G. J. (1995). *The Vandals' Crown.* Free Press.

Perkins, J. (2004). *Confessions of an Economic Hit Man.*

---

[i] http://www.palagems.com/choosing_an_appraiser.htm

[ii] http://dictionary.reference.com/browse/mart Definition of "Mart"

[iii] https://en.wikipedia.org/wiki/Reality-based_community

[iv] https://en.wikipedia.org/wiki/Fiat_money Fiat Money explanation

[v] http://www.federalreserve.gov/faqs/currency_12771.htm Cost of printing US Currency

[vi] http://watchingamerica.com/WA/2015/06/18/bush-family-buy-up-guarani-aquifer/

[vii] http://granews.info/content/paraguay-cia-behind-coup

[viii] http://www.globalresearch.ca/us-sponsored-institutional-coup-in-paraguay-back-to-the-cia-s-good-old-days/31905

[ix] http://www.rferl.org/content/article/1095057.html

[x] https://en.wikipedia.org/wiki/Sharia Sharia Law

[xi] https://en.wikipedia.org/wiki/Riba Riba or interest according to Sharia Law

[xii] https://en.wikipedia.org/wiki/Military_payment_certificate What are Military Payment Certificates

[xiii] http://www.investopedia.com/ask/answers/09/trading-the-cable.asp

[xiv] https://en.wikipedia.org/wiki/King_Cotton

xv https://en.wikipedia.org/wiki/Nixon_Shock Nixon Shock

xvi http://www.presidency.ucsb.edu/ws/index.php?pid=59049&st=&st1=

xvii https://en.wikipedia.org/wiki/History_of_Russia#Early_history

xviii https://mises.org/library/inflation-and-fall-roman-empire
Mises article: Inflation and the fall of the Roman Empire

xix http://www.zerohedge.com/news/2015-12-08/american-forex-delusion

xx https://en.wikipedia.org/wiki/Banking_in_the_United_States

xxi http://www.history.com/news/8-things-you-may-not-know-about-american-money

xxii http://www.theatlantic.com/business/archive/2014/03/yes-the-fed-makes-comic-books/284200/

xxiii http://www.independent.co.uk/news/uk/home-news/the-rothschild-libel-why-has-it-taken-200-years-for-an-anti-semitic-slur-that-emerged-from-the-10216101.html

xxiv https://en.wikipedia.org/wiki/Pigeon_racing

xxv http://www.hereinreality.com/insidertrading.html#.VsiXk_krKJA

xxvi http://www.wsj.com/articles/banks-civil-forex-settlements-near-2-billion-1434541324

xxvii http://financial.thomsonreuters.com/content/dam/openweb/documents/pdf/financial/ultra-low-latency-economic-indicators.pdf

xxviii http://www.federalreserve.gov/faqs/about_14986.htm
About the Federal Reserve

xxix http://www.cftc.gov/index.htm Commodity Futures Trading Commission CFTC Website

xxx https://en.wikipedia.org/wiki/Dodd%E2%80%93Frank_Wall_Street_Reform_and_Consumer_Protection_Act

xxxi http://www.cftc.gov/idc/groups/public/@lrfederalregister/documents/file/2010-21729a.pdf

xxxii https://assets.documentcloud.org/documents/1363910/senate-report-on-wall-st-s-role-in-commodities.pdf

xxxiii http://www.bloomberg.com/news/articles/2014-11-13/forex-investors-may-face-1-billion-loss-as-trade-site-vanishes xxxiv https://en.wikipedia.org/wiki/Big_Mac_Index Measure of purchasing power parity via Big Mac Hamburger Sandwich from McDonalds

xxxv http://corpgov.law.harvard.edu/2012/12/24/personal-jurisdiction-over-non-u-s-financial-institutions/

xxxvi https://history.state.gov/historicaldocuments/frus1969-76v31/d63

xxxvii http://www.reuters.com/article/usa-fed-shift-idUSL1N0W70U320150305

xxxviii https://en.wikipedia.org/wiki/Executive_Order_6102

xxxix http://www.zerohedge.com/article/its-official-america-now-enforces-capital-controls

xl http://www.swissinfo.ch/eng/cia-has-access-to-swiss-transactions/5282872

xli

http://www.wsj.com/articles/SB10001424052970204257504577150460936873268

xlii https://www.bis.org/about/index.htm

xliii https://www.bis.org/about/chronology.htm

xliv http://www.pca-cpa.org/

xlv https://en.wikipedia.org/wiki/Eurodollar

xlvi https://en.wikipedia.org/wiki/Forex_scandal WM/Reuters Forex Market Rigging Scandal

xlvii http://eliteeservices.blogspot.com/2016/02/5-most-galling-lines-from-barclays.html

xlviii https://en.wikipedia.org/wiki/Pujo_Committee

xlix http://www.hausfeld.com/news/us/hausfeld-announces-settlement-with-bank-of-america-in-foreign-exchange-anti

l http://www.ccfsettlement.com/faqs/amex/

li https://en.wikipedia.org/wiki/Rai_stones Largest physical currency in the world

lii https://www.foreignaffairs.com/articles/united-states/2014-08-11/print-less-transfer-more

liii http://positivemoney.org/2014/09/central-banks-give-money-directly-people/

liv http://www.washingtonsblog.com/2013/06/81-5-of-money-created-through-quantitative-easing-is-sitting-there-gathering-dust-instead-of-helping-the-economy.html

lv http://www.huffingtonpost.com/robert-auerbach/massive-misconceptions-ab_b_3490373.html

lvi

https://www.frbservices.org/serviceofferings/access/index.html Federal Reserve Bank Services lvii http://dailyreckoning.com/fed-banker-in-charge-of-qe-says-qe-is-abysmal-failure/

lviii https://www.fbi.gov/newyork/press-releases/2012/manhattan-u.s.-attorney-and-fbi-assistant-director-in-charge-announce-arrest-of-computer-programmer-for-stealing-proprietary-code-from-the-federal-reserve-bank-of-new-york

lix http://www.jekyllislandhistory.com/federalreserve.shtml

lx http://www.publiceye.org/conspire/flaherty/flaherty1.html

lxi https://www.newyorkfed.org/markets/liquidity_swap.html

lxii
http://www.federalreserve.gov/monetarypolicy/bst_openmarketops.htm

lxiii http://blogs.wsj.com/moneybeat/2015/01/16/six-in-ten-retail-forex-traders-lose-money-each-quarter/

lxiv http://www.bloombergview.com/quicktake/the-london-whale

lxv https://en.wikipedia.org/wiki/Hyperinflation_in_Zimbabwe

lxvi https://en.wikipedia.org/wiki/The_World_Is_Flat

lxvii http://jalopnik.com/5782082/the-strange-link-between-samurai-swords-and-japans-nuclear-reactors

lxviii https://www.iridium.com/products/details/iridiumextreme
Rugged phones that will work under any conditions

lxix
http://www.imf.org/external/np/exr/center/mm/eng/mm_sc_03.htm Triffin Dilemma

lxx http://www.frommers.com/destinations/cuba/777910

lxxi http://www.bloomberg.com/news/articles/2015-04-16/german-bonds-average-yield-turns-negative-as-ecb-spurs-buyers

lxxii https://en.wikipedia.org/wiki/Nonfarm_payrolls NFP

lxxiii http://www.shadowstats.com/ Website about government's incorrect stats

lxxiv http://data.bls.gov/timeseries/LNS14000000

lxxv http://www.zerohedge.com/news/2015-09-04/record-94-million-americans-not-labor-force-participation-rate-lowest-1977 Real unemployment rate

lxxvi
https://www.frbatlanta.org/chcs/LaborForceParticipation.aspx

lxxvii http://www.zerohedge.com/news/2015-03-30/qe-people-what-could-go-wrong

lxxviii http://www.thestreet.com/story/13472874/1/herbalife-ltd-announces-fourth-quarter-and-full-year-2015-results.html HFA financial release

lxxix http://www.equilar.com/reports/17-100-largest-company-CEOs-2015.html Top CEO pay

lxxx https://www.geico.com/more/saving/insurance-101/unusual-insurance-policies/ Alien Abduction Insurance

lxxxi https://www.sec.gov/rules/final/2010/33-9142.pdf

lxxxii https://www.fbi.gov/boston/press-releases/2014/former-owner-of-trading-company-pleads-guilty-to-multi-million-dollar-fraud-scheme

lxxxiii https://www.atcbrokers.com/ ATC Brokers

lxxxiv https://www.tradecrowd.com/learn-to-trade/strategies/top-5-forex-traders-ever/

lxxxv http://www.reuters.com/article/us-forex-hedgefunds-idUSBRE9BI0P720131219

lxxxvi http://www.reuters.com/article/us-forex-hedgefunds-idUSBRE9BI0P720131219

lxxxvii https://en.wikipedia.org/wiki/James_Harris_Simons

lxxxviii

http://www.nfa.futures.org/BasicNet/CaseDocument.aspx?seqnum=3841

lxxxix

http://money.cnn.com/2011/09/21/news/economy/federal_reserve_operation_twist/

xc http://www.zerohedge.com/news/2015-11-05/play-forex-fix-jpy-and-chf-pairs-range-bound

xci http://www.reuters.com/article/us-markets-forex-fxcm-idUSKBN0JU2G720141217

xcii https://en.wikipedia.org/wiki/Sharpe_ratio

xciii http://www.finalternatives.com/node/542

xciv https://en.wikipedia.org/wiki/Amaranth_Advisors Large institutional hedge fund collapse

xcv http://www-03.ibm.com/systems/z/solutions/banking.html

xcvi

https://en.wikipedia.org/wiki/Financial_Information_eXchange trading communications

xcvii http://www.oanda.com/forex-trading/analysis/open-position-ratios

xcviii

http://www.cftc.gov/MARKETREPORTS/COMMITMENTSOFTRADERS/INDEX.HTM

xcix https://en.wikipedia.org/wiki/Gambler%27s_ruin Common problem traders face

c https://en.wikipedia.org/wiki/Carl_von_Clausewitz Western version of Sun Tzu
ci https://en.wikipedia.org/wiki/Game_theory
cii https://www.quandl.com/collections/futures/cme-euro-fx-futures Euro FX Futures Contract
ciii https://www.google.com/finance?q=NYSEARCA:UUP
civ http://www.investopedia.com/articles/active-trading/041414/use-knockout-options-lower-cost-hedging.asp
cv http://blogs.wsj.com/marketbeat/2010/02/17/goldman-and-greece-what-the-heck-are-currency-swaps/
cvi https://t0.com/ The trade IS the settlement
cvii http://www.benzinga.com/analyst-ratings/analyst-color/16/02/6248774/russian-hackers-illegally-manipulated-400-million-of-dol#/ixzz40NkKb9XZ
cviii https://www.irs.gov/uac/Newsroom/IRS-Virtual-Currency-Guidance
cix https://en.wikipedia.org/wiki/Local_currency
cx http://www.coindesk.com/new-york-bitcoin-scene-divided-as-bitlicense-deadline-looms/
cxi http://www.scstatehouse.gov/sess119_2011-2012/bills/500.htm
cxii https://en.wikipedia.org/wiki/South_Carolina_pound Currency used in South Carolina issued by the state of South Carolina
cxiii https://en.wikipedia.org/wiki/Greek_withdrawal_from_the_eurozone
cxiv https://en.wikipedia.org/wiki/List_of_circulating_currencies 180 Total circulating currencies in the world
cxv http://usatoday30.usatoday.com/news/world/2009-03-31-petro-currency_N.htm Hugo Chavez proposes "Petro Currency"
cxvi https://en.wikipedia.org/wiki/Category:Proposed_currencies List of 17 proposed currencies
cxvii https://fortresscapitalinc.com/2016/03/24/swiss-national-bank-admits-it-spent-470-billion-on-currency-manipulation-since-2010/

Made in the USA
Middletown, DE
22 August 2017